"Founding a global ministry probably I didn't have a godly wife who knows ... .. pray, and it would not have expanded as far as it has without an army of intercessors. Sue Detweiler is a godly wife with many years of ministry experience who knows how to communicate with her heavenly Father. I would encourage you to read this book and become an intercessor for your family, your church, and God's kingdom."

—Dr. Neil T. Anderson, founder and president emeritus,
Freedom in Christ Ministries

"Sue Detweiler is simply extraordinary! A gifted woman of God who serves with both grace and godly wisdom, she is a person of courage, integrity, transparency, and faithfulness to the call of the Lord in her life. She sees beyond what may seem to be the impossible and goes forward in Christ, realizing that *His* promise makes all things possible through prayer! Having known Sue for more than fifteen years, I have developed a deep respect for her zeal for the Lord, her family, the lost, and the extended body of Christ. The Lord has called Sue to great significance and purpose."

—Glenn C. Burris, president, The Foursquare Church

"If there is one thing I know about Sue Detweiler, it is that she is a woman of fierce faith. Her passion for God and her desire for women to live with confidence, boldness, and grace is core to who she is and oozes from the pages of this book. Grounded in Scripture and complemented by personal stories, *Women Who Move Mountains* will inspire and provoke you to be all God has designed you to be."

—Jenni Catron, leadership coach and author,
The 4 Dimensions of Extraordinary Leadership

"This comprehensive manual will greatly help the reader to understand the character and ways of God."

—Joy Dawson, international Bible teacher,
author, and YWAM missionary

"We are never finished when it comes to learning about prayer. There is always something new and fresh God wants to teach us. In her engaging book *Women Who Move Mountains*, Sue Detweiler reminds us of the transforming power of prayer and the joy of humbly coming to God in every area of our lives. This heart-lifting book will refresh your prayer life and take you deeper still in what the Bible has to teach us about prayer."

—Karol Ladd, author,
The Power of a Positive Woman

"Sue Detweiler has written a life-transforming book. The stories of amazing women who have overcome many obstacles by the power of God truly touched my heart. The theme of knowing God intimately recurs in each chapter as she lays out biblical principles and practical applications. *Women Who Move Mountains* is a must-read for everyone who desires to know God more intimately."

—Suellen Roberts, founder and president,
Christian Women in Media Association

"A passionate invitation to become part of the crowd that cares about knowing the person and power of God in practical ways that transform, heal, and make all things new. Say yes and be awed by the treasure you discover along the way."

—Pam Vredevelt, licensed professional counselor; inspirational speaker; and author, *Empty Arms Journal*

"Praying in faith moves fear and obstacles away so prayers can be offered to God fervently and with the assurance that they will be answered. We all need this masterpiece!"

—Thelma Wells, DD, president and CEO, A Woman of God Ministries; author; speaker; professor; and founder, Generation Love-Divine Explosion Conferences

WOMEN

Who Move

MOUNTAINS

WOMEN
Who Move
MOUNTAINS

praying with confidence,
boldness, and grace

SUE DETWEILER

BETHANYHOUSE

a division of Baker Publishing Group
Minneapolis, Minnesota

Published by Bethany House Publishers
11400 Hampshire Avenue South
Bloomington, Minnesota 55438
www.bethanyhouse.com

Bethany House Publishers is a division of
Baker Publishing Group, Grand Rapids, Michigan

Printed in the United States of America

Library of Congress Cataloging-in-Publication Data
Names: Detweiler, Sue, author.
Title: Women who move mountains : praying with confidence, boldness, and grace
 / Sue Detweiler.
Description: Minneapolis, Minnesota : Bethany House, 2017. | Includes
 bibliographical references.
Identifiers: LCCN 2016050056 | ISBN 9780764219146 (trade paper : alk. paper)
Subjects: LCSH: Christian women—Religious life. | Prayer—Christianity.
Classification: LCC BV4527 .D48 2017 | DDC 248.8/43—dc23
LC record available at https://lccn.loc.gov/2016050056

Emphasis in Scripture shown by italics is the author's.

Cover design by Brand Navigation

Author is represented by Greg Johnson at WordServe Literary Group.

17 18 19 20 21 22 23   9 8 7 6 5 4 3

To Joy Dawson, who inspired me to have an
intimate friendship with God.

To Jack Hayford, who taught me that prayer
is invading the impossible.

To Tom White, who inspired me to recognize spiritual attack and fight for unity.

To Larry Lea, who empowered me to pray
the Lord's Prayer.

To Stormie Omartian, who taught me
the power of being a praying woman.

To Neil Anderson, who showed me a path of
deliverance and freedom in Christ.

To Dutch Sheets, who taught me how to pray
with power and purpose.

To Bill Johnson, who inspired me to pray for
heaven to invade earth.

To all the amazing women I've met,
and those I haven't, who pray with
confidence, boldness, and grace.

CONTENTS

FOREWORD

I love mountains and I love climbing them! I can't remember a time when I didn't relish the adventure of being out in nature and the challenge of getting to the top. In recent years, my love for climbing has taken me to the top of Mount Kilimanjaro (19,341 ft.) in Africa and Everest Base Camp (17,598 ft.) in Nepal. High elevation trekking is one of the hardest but most thrilling things I've ever done.

But what do we do when those mountains are not just for climbing, but they are very real obstacles, hindrances, or problems blocking our way forward—blocking the blessings that God has stored up for us but that seem impossible to grasp because of the mountain or mountains in our way.

We do what Jesus said we should do. We tell the mountain to MOVE!

Jesus said, "If you have faith as small as a mustard seed, you can say to this mountain, 'Move from here to there,' and it will move. Nothing will be impossible for you" (Matthew 17:20 NIV).

Years ago, I was in line for a position I'd hoped and prayed would open up. When the job finally became available, I was sure they'd pick me! I felt it was a perfect fit for me, but no call came. But God in His mercy gave me a vision. I saw a large pile of debris like you'd see after a storm (twigs and tree limbs) piled twelve feet high and twelve feet wide. It was totally impenetrable.

Somehow, I knew exactly what the vision meant! There was something blocking me from this position, something hindering management from seeing me in this role.

I knew I had to pray and tell it to move. Although I felt a little ridiculous, I called a friend and asked if she'd join me to move a mountain out of my way. After dark, we met outside the building, and we prophetically pushed that pile of debris out of the way. We declared it done and no longer able to hinder God's perfect will for me. The very next morning I got the call—and I got the job! And the rest is history.

In *Women Who Move Mountains,* Sue Detweiler takes us on a journey, where we learn to speak to the mountains of fear, discouragement, loss, pain, or whatever it is that's hindering us from moving forward with God, and then watch it move in the name of Jesus! You have the power. It only takes a mustard seed of faith. The same God who made the mountains and made them for climbing gave us the power to move them by our prayers! So get your hiking boots on because you're about ready to climb higher with your Savior than you've ever been and see for yourself that with God, you too can move mountains!

—Wendy Griffith, *700 Club* co-host, author,
and mountain climber

ACKNOWLEDGMENTS

I want to take this opportunity to thank my family. To my husband, Wayne, for the freedom and encouragement to share this message. To my children, Rachel Joy, Angela Grace, Hannah Elizabeth, Sarah Faith, Alexandre Joel, Ezequiel Paul, and sons-in-love, Dustin Wayne and Christopher Bryan, who have inspired so many hours on my knees in prayer and joy-filled laughter at God's answers. To my first grandson, Andrew Wayne—marked by love, cherished by family, and chosen by God—may you grow to be a man who moves mountains through prayer. To my dad, Allen, who inspired me to write, and my mom, Donna, who taught me to pray boldly. To my extended family, who walk in faith and prayer on a daily basis.

I want to thank those in the body of Christ who have taught me to pray: Joy Dawson, Jack Hayford, Tom White, Larry Lea, Stormie Omartian, Neil Anderson, Dutch Sheets, Bill Johnson, Jim Goll, Glenn Burris, Dale Evrist, Toni Kline, David Coffey, Kim Pitner, and so many more intercessors and friends who have labored long hours in prayer.

I want to thank Kim Bangs, Shaun Tabatt, Grace Kasper, Ellen Chalifoux, and the Bethany House team for making this book a reality, as well as my friend Rhonda Robinson, who shared her story and read and reread this manuscript to help fine-tune the message and help me birth it. I also want to thank Amy, Ann, Brigitte, Donna, Hannah, Lori, Marta, Marti, and Mary for transparently sharing their stories of how God brought healing through prayer. Thank you to the pastors, leaders, and intercessors around the world who pray daily with confidence, boldness, and grace.

PART ONE

Introduction

You Are Invited on a Prayer Journey

Every journey has a beginning. The starting point of prayer is God. Like a father who waits to hear every detail of your life, He waits for you. You don't need to get dressed up and go to church to reverently pray. The God of the universe invites you to come as you are. You can endure anything when you are at God's side. He is the transformer. He turns sorrow to joy. He turns bitter to sweet.

As you come close to God in prayer, He brings purpose even from the brokenness of your life. You can't remain downcast when you turn your face upward to God. He reaches down to your lowest pit, but He doesn't leave you there.

> So many are saying, "God will never rescue him!" But you, O Lord, are a shield around me; you are my glory, the one who holds my head high. I cried out to the Lord, and he answered me from his holy mountain.
>
> Psalm 3:2–4

Negative thoughts may try to convince you that God will never rescue you. Prayer rinses these plaguing doubts from your mind. As you cry out to God, He answers you. He shields you with His presence. The more you know God, the more you trust Him. You no longer feel like you need to be perfect. You learn how to come into His presence. You begin the joyful pursuit of God.

You Are Invited to Become a Woman Who Moves Mountains

When I am standing next to a mountain, I feel small and insignificant. It towers over me with immovable fortitude. Jesus used this picture to call us to increased faith. He said,

> "Have faith in God," Jesus answered. "Truly I tell you, if anyone says to this mountain, 'Go, throw yourself into the sea,' and does not doubt in their heart but believes that what they say will happen, it will be done for them. Therefore I tell you, whatever you ask for in prayer, believe that you have received it, and it will be yours."
>
> Mark 11:22–24 NIV

To pray with this mountain-moving faith challenges each one of us to overcome the obstacles in our lives and make them opportunities of purposeful mission. It requires each of us to move out of our comfort zone, have faith in God, and speak to every mountain that separates us from God and His assignment in our lives.

Often the very barrier that has been used by the Enemy to stop our progress becomes the stepping-stone to grow in greater intimacy with Him. We grow stronger as we push against the resistance. Our spiritual muscles are exercised as we triumph over the plans of the Enemy.

You Are Invited to Be a Fellow Traveler

Just by picking up this book and beginning to read you are joining a whole company of women who are learning to pray with *confidence, boldness,* and *grace.* This book about prayer will not be ritualistic lists of do's and don'ts. It is about being real and raw with God, learning to uncover the weak parts of your life and receive His strength. It's about choosing to bring your wounded areas to Him and receive His healing.

When you remove these barriers that block the fulfillment of your destiny, you will grow closer to God and others. Many women want to be free but don't know how to be free. This book provides a step-by-step journey to finding true freedom in Christ.

The odd-numbered chapters explain how to transform your relationship with God and give examples of biblical and modern women who have moved mountains in prayer. The even-numbered chapters show how to apply these prayer principles to your own life as you discover the truth of God's Word. You may want to write your personal answers to these questions in your own journal or go to www.SueDetweiler.com to download bonus journal pages.

Removing barriers between us and God improves our prayer lives. That's what this book will do for you!

This book is for you if . . .

You are just starting your journey with God. . . .
You are a longtime traveler with God, but you want more. . . .
You want relationship, not religion in your prayer life. . . .
You want to pray, but you sometimes feel stuck. . . .
You desire greater transformation in the
broken places of your life. . . .
You want to be healed. . . .
You want to be whole. . . .
You want to know God intimately. . . .
You want a new beginning in your life. . . .
You want to be real, not fake in your prayer life. . . .
You want to go deeper. . . .
You want to find purpose. . . .
You want a fresh start. . . .

You Are Invited to Begin a Women's Prayer Group

We need to encourage each other in our lives of prayer. We may glance at someone else and think their time with God must be more incredible than our own. If we are honest, no one's perfect, but everyone is on a life journey. Christian women are fellow travelers with our sisters around the world. Our hope is not in learning a new method of prayer. It is in knowing the person and power of Jesus Christ.

As we travel together you will experience . . .

A new beginning in prayer . . .
A greater understanding of your calling to pray . . .
A stronger relationship with God, who is calling you to pray . . .
A fresh inspiration and momentum to pray . . .
A transformation of your broken places through prayer . . .
A significant increase in your intimacy with God
through prayer . . .
A genuine depth and purpose in prayer . . .
A greater knowledge of God's Word about prayer . . .
A clear understanding of God's ways through prayer . . .
A readiness to pray . . .

Consider meeting with a group of women and discussing this book and praying for each other. The power of prayer is multiplied when two or three gather together in agreement. Complete the assigned chapters prior to your women's group.

The format of your group can be simple:

- Ten minutes: Opening icebreaker (download icebreaker questions at www.SueDetweiler.com).
- Five minutes: Watch bonus video for chapter.
- Thirty minutes: Discuss the group questions and reflect on how the chapters impact each of you personally.
- Fifteen minutes: Pray for each other.

If you are a group leader and would like to watch a leader training video, go to www.SueDetweiler.com.

The schedule of your group could be as follows:

- Week 1: Read chapter 1 and complete questions in chapter 2.
- Week 2: Read chapter 3 and complete questions in chapter 4.
- Week 3: Read chapter 5 and complete questions in chapter 6.
- Week 4: Read chapter 7 and complete questions in chapter 8.
- Week 5: Read chapter 9 and complete questions in chapter 10.
- Week 6: Read chapter 11 and complete questions in chapter 12.
- Week 7: Read chapter 13 and complete questions in chapter 14.
- Week 8: Read chapter 15 and complete questions in chapter 16.
- Week 9: Read chapter 17 and complete questions in chapter 18.
- Week 10: Read chapter 19 and complete questions in chapter 20.
- **Bonus:** After you have completed this women's study, throw a party and invite friends. Share personal testimonies of what God has done in your life as you have become *Women Who Move Mountains.*

Believe God for His Transformation in Your Life

Our confidence is in God. He is the One who has led you to pick up this book as a tool in His hands to transform you. It's the great exchange! He replaces your worst with His best. Remember, in order to move mountains in your own life, you need to have faith in God and speak to that mountain and watch it move. So let's begin right now.

Stand up wherever you are in the world and pray this prayer out loud with confidence, boldness, and grace.

All-powerful God,
I begin this journey with expectation. You are a mountain-moving God. I choose to change the way I think, speak, and act as I apply the transformative truth of your Word to my life. I choose

to trust you with the broken places of my heart. I give you my disappointment and I receive your hope. I place my confidence in you. You lead me and guide me. I open my heart to allow you to use the simple words of this book and the power of your Word to transform me. Merciful God, lead me to the home of your healing heart so I can share your heart with others. In Jesus' name, amen.

— 1 —

I Believe

Transforming Fear into Faith

The Prayer of Desperation

"Get my baby out!" I screamed with a raspy voice. My desperate pleas for help were barely heard. Smoke filled the room as the cries of my newborn awakened me into a living nightmare. The house was on fire, and I couldn't get out.

As a young girl, my mind would wonder, *What would I do if my house caught on fire?* Then I would create a very clear, level-headed plan. However, smoke inhalation disorients your brain.

The sounds of my precious five-week-old daughter's wails pierced my sleep. Walking to her bedroom in the dark, half-asleep, to feed her every night had never been a problem. Now, suddenly, I was lost and couldn't find her doorway.

I clawed at the clothes in my closet trying to find my way out. Then, stumbling in the other direction, I felt the windowpane. It wasn't until I opened the window and looked out that I realized my house was on fire. I tried to scream for help, but no one could hear my cries.

I collapsed. In desperation, I prayed the prayer everyone prays when they think they are about to die—*"Help!"* My daughter and I would have died that night if my husband hadn't gotten home in time. Imagine his horror when he rounded the corner and could see the sky lit up by orange flames.

Cars and people filled our street, watching in horror. The home next to us, which was under construction, had already burned to the ground. A home on the other side stood engulfed in a raging inferno. The family of four stood huddled together, watching all of their belongings turn to ash.

There was only one fire truck on the scene. The other fire trucks sat motionless, waiting for a passing train. My husband grabbed the arm of the fireman. Frantically he asked, "Did you get my wife and baby out?" The fireman dropped the hose and together they ran to the front door. The neighbors had assumed we were still on vacation. They didn't realize we were trapped inside.

When I heard someone coming into our home, I began to scream hysterically, "Get my baby out!" I don't remember what the fireman who saved my life looked like. I just remember him holding his flashlight up and saying, "Come toward the light." I made my way toward what looked like a tiny pin-light in the smothering darkness. At last, I felt his arms as he led me out to safety.[1]

Come toward the Light

Have you ever found yourself in a dark place, not knowing which direction to go? It's in the blackest night that light pierces the darkness. Come toward the light. Prayer brings light to your path so that you know which way to go. Prayer taps into God's power to transform your daily life. God is all-sufficient, all-knowing, and all-powerful. God is not only able to change situations, He is willing to change them.

24

The main way we connect with God's will for our lives is through prayer.

God is not an abusive, negligent dad who will scold you if you don't pray correctly. God is the ever-present, always-available Maker of heaven and earth. It is in His presence that there is fullness of joy. Coming toward the light is a simple thing that a child can do. In fact, Jesus encouraged us to come to God like children.

> But Jesus called the children to him and said, "Let the little children come to me, and do not hinder them, for the kingdom of God belongs to such as these. Truly I tell you, anyone who will not receive the kingdom of God like a little child will never enter it."
>
> Luke 18:16–17 NIV

Childlike hope spurs us on to discovery. Like a child, we can look to God's light, trusting that He is leading us. He is not going to leave us. We enter into His kingdom as children. It's when we come to the end of ourselves that we find God. He is the source of our life. He is the Maker of heaven and earth. He created you in His image. He gave you life, breath, and purpose.

If you are trying to walk through life without the help of God, you will be lonely, depressed, and overwhelmed. But if you are ready to find help, He is waiting to help you. He is ready to pour His life-giving, life-altering, life-changing power into you. He will replace your desperation with hope.

A Mother's Prayers

We spent a long, weary night in the hospital as the doctors examined and treated my baby and me for smoke inhalation. In the early hours of the morning we called my mom. That's when we had the conversation that forever changed my perspective on prayer.

"Mom, we're all right." The long pause of silence was deafening.

Finally, she spoke: "What happened?"

Wayne described the huge fire and how there was only one fire truck, leaving three homes devastated. The heat from the blazing inferno melted a car bumper and the shutters of our neighbors' home. People lined the street as the fire lit up the night sky. As we told Mom about the fire, her quiet peace engulfed our stress.

"You're the ones I have been praying for," she said. The month before, my mom began to meditate, fast, and pray over Isaiah 43:

> When you pass through the waters, I will be with you;
> and when you pass through the rivers, they will not sweep
>   over you.
> *When you walk through the fire, you will not be burned;*
> *the flames will not set you ablaze.*
>
> Isaiah 43:2 NIV

Later I would look back on this telephone conversation and marvel at the power of prayer and the peace of my own mother. I would realize that prayer is a matter of life and death. I would rejoice in how God saved us from the fire. I would celebrate—just like Shadrach, Meshach, and Abednego—that God was with me in the fire. I would wonder at how the bondages of my life were burned up and I was set free. (See Daniel 3.)

However, my present reality was far from tranquil. My whole life-system was on overload. *I had no home . . . no baby furniture . . . no diapers . . . no clothes . . .*

As we walked into the shell of our home, trying to salvage things, my emotions were more charred than the black soot that blanketed every surface. The neighbors rallied and helped with our physical needs, but I was a mess. The only prayer I continued to pray was *"Help!"*

If you are in this place of desperation right now, lean into the wisdom of sisters and brothers who will hold up your arms in prayer. It's okay to not be okay. All of us have times when our lives are falling apart. God will prompt people to pray for you and help you carry your burden.

Coming toward the light of Jesus will bring peace to your heart and mind. You don't have to have everything figured out. You just need to know the One who holds the world together—Jesus!

Jesus, born a baby in a manger, who grew to be a man, knows your pain and loss. He walked on this earth and suffered and died for us. God chose for His son to be born at a time in history when there would be no room in the inn. God chose for Jesus to be born of a virgin girl named Mary.

Mary, the Mother of Jesus

In the first picture I saw of Mary, the mother of Jesus, she had light surrounding her. We make fun of the old-fashioned paintings with halos, but now I realize that the artist is trying to paint on canvas what they sense. Mary was surrounded by light because she was in God's presence.

Mary was a girl from Nazareth. In the Bible, we see things about her character that got the attention of God himself. It wasn't unusual for a young girl to be a virgin, but it was amazing to be chosen by God to bear His one and only Son. When the angel first appeared to Mary, she was afraid. Gabriel said,

> "Greetings, favored woman! The Lord is with you!" Confused and disturbed, Mary tried to think what the angel could mean. "Don't be afraid, Mary," the angel told her, "for you have found favor with God! You will conceive and give birth to a son, and you will name him Jesus."
>
> Luke 1:28–31

Fear could have gripped Mary so tight that she wouldn't have been able to hear the angel's words. But Mary didn't let fear stop her from a fresh encounter. She was confused, but she wanted to understand. This "good news" that the angel brought was life altering. Every Jewish woman in Israel wanted the joy and privilege of being the mother of the Messiah. But no virgin wanted to be pregnant illegitimately. Mary asked the angel,

"But how can this happen? I am a virgin." The angel replied, "The Holy Spirit will come upon you, and the power of the Most High will overshadow you. So the baby to be born will be holy, and he will be called the Son of God."

Luke 1:34–35

How would you have handled the angel's answer? He was giving an explanation that was impossible. It had never happened before and hasn't happened since. Would your heart rise up to trust God and receive His Word like Mary did?

Here's how Mary responded: "'I am the Lord's servant. May everything you have said about me come true.' And then the angel left her" (Luke 1:38).

Mary's response holds the key to why she was favored by God. In the depths of her heart, she was God's servant. She rose up in faith to believe that God can do the impossible. She didn't argue. She didn't resist. She didn't point out all the reasons that it couldn't or shouldn't happen. She simply opened her hands and her heart to receive the gift, and honor, of bearing God's Son.

Mary quietly pondered God's word to her. She prayed and remembered that the angel had mentioned her relative Elizabeth. The angel had said that the impossible was about to happen in her life as well. The angel said,

What's more, your relative Elizabeth has become pregnant in her old age! People used to say she was barren, but she has conceived a son and is now in her sixth month. For the word of God will never fail.

Luke 1:36–37

Within a few days, Mary found a way to travel to see Elizabeth. She was older and wiser and able to comfort Mary about the amazing miracle. Elizabeth had known the painful shame of being barren. Zechariah had been unable to speak after his angelic encounter in the temple. His fear turned to faith as he came home and somehow communicated with Elizabeth what God had said.

The confirmation was the miracle that at a very old age, Elizabeth was pregnant with Zechariah's child.

Our faith is strengthened through answered prayer. The prayer Zechariah and Elizabeth had carried together as a couple was a sweet fragrance to God, who saw their obedience but also knew the right time for John the Baptist to be conceived. John was to be the forerunner to Jesus' coming on this earth. Even in Elizabeth's womb, John preceded Jesus.

Mary rushes up the hill to Elizabeth, wanting not only her comfort but also confirmation that it was God at work in her.

> At the sound of Mary's greeting, Elizabeth's child leaped within her, and Elizabeth was filled with the Holy Spirit. Elizabeth gave a glad cry and exclaimed to Mary, "God has blessed you above all women, and your child is blessed. Why am I so honored, that the mother of my Lord should visit me? When I heard your greeting, the baby in my womb jumped for joy. You are blessed because you believed that the Lord would do what he said."
>
> Luke 1:41–45

This prophetic word spoken by Elizabeth to Mary broke the silence of 400 years, when there were no prophetic words spoken between the Old Testament and the New Testament. Elizabeth was able to see the joy and honor with which Mary was blessed. Elizabeth understood exactly why Mary was blessed. It was because she believed that the Lord would do what He said.

Fear Puts God on Trial

Mary believed and was blessed by God. She didn't blame God. She didn't become fearful and back away from her calling. She pressed through the difficulty and embraced faith.

When we are fearful or anxious, we are declaring that we can't fully trust God to care about the details of our lives. Fear, anxiety, and intimidation are part of the Enemy's family. Satan's plan is that you will be constantly stressed, uncertain, and hesitant about your daily life. He traps you with your desire to please people more than God.

Mary cared more about what God thought than the opinions of those around her. She didn't allow the poison of fear to block her call. She fought the battle of fear by choosing God's perspective on how to think and speak about her situation.

If we don't replace fear with faith, we will be led down the dangerous path of unbelief and disobedience. Unbelief accuses God at His very essence. It puts God on trial to prove himself while denying the undeniable evidence all around.

To engage in prayer is to declare war on the demonic forces of fear that accuse God. These accusations can come as subtle thoughts against the power of God. Fear will manifest in us as insecurity, concern, despair, doubt, dread, horror, panic, agitation, unease, fright, and even terror.

If you are struggling with some sort of fear in your life, you can know without a doubt that fear has come from the Enemy.

> For this reason I remind you to fan into flame the gift of God, which is in you through the laying on of my hands. For the Spirit God gave us does not make us timid, but gives us power, love and self-discipline.
>
> 2 Timothy 1:6–7 NIV

Many of us do not fulfill the call of God on our lives because we are chained to fear. Every time we try to move forward, the devil uses fear to try to stop us. Fear will make you want to stand still. Fear accuses God for every difficult thing you have experienced in your life. We let fear have power over us when we try to protect ourselves so we don't experience pain. The fear of lack, fear of failure, fear of rejection, fear of abandonment all take hold in our lives if we haven't thoroughly invited God in to help us overcome emotional pain and loss.

You and I need to learn to step out and obey God in spite of our fear. Sometimes, you have to do what God says even when you feel afraid.

Replacing Fear with Faith

We don't have a *fear* problem; we have a *faith* problem. It's not about fearing less; it's about believing more. If your goal is to have a fear-free life, you will be disappointed or your life will become small. Fear will be the boundary of your existence.

We replace fear with faith every time we make a decision to trust God in our daily lives. Replacing fear with faith is a moment-by-moment choice to anchor our confidence in Jesus. You may not feel 100 percent free from fear, but little by little, as you step out in faith, you will see God work miracles in your life.

The holy moment when Mary said yes to God's call, she was taking a step of faith. She did not know every difficulty she would experience in being Jesus' mother. Still, she made a choice to trust God. She felt all the same feelings of anxiety, fear, and worry that every adolescent girl struggles with. What made her unique and favored was that she didn't allow her feelings to overshadow her faith and trust in God. She was able to privately ponder God's word to her before it was evident that she was pregnant.

Not long after Mary returned to Nazareth, it probably became clear that she was pregnant. Just by walking through the village, she was in danger of being dragged outside the city and having stones thrown at her until she died. The rejection and suspicion were inevitable. Again, Mary had faith in God.

Mary was engaged to be married to a kind man named Joseph. As her fiancé, Joseph did not want to disgrace Mary publicly, so he decided to quietly break the engagement. But before he could take action on his plan, an angel appeared to him in a dream and said,

> "Joseph, son of David," the angel said, "do not be afraid to take Mary as your wife. For the child within her was conceived by the Holy Spirit. And she will have a son, and you are to name him Jesus, for he will save his people from their sins."
>
> Matthew 1:20–21

Joseph, in many ways, is the hero in this story. He stepped up and shielded Mary (and Jesus) from harm. He protected her. He took her as his wife but did not have sexual relations with her until after Jesus was born.

Learning to Pray

It's easy to see why Mary has been revered by so many. Her faith-filled response to God is amazing. She didn't argue or fight with His word. There is nothing recorded to show that she became angry or blamed God for her rejection. Beginning this book with Mary the mother of Jesus as our example is intimidating.

When my house was on fire, I didn't have a halo over my head as I prayed for help. But I did have fire over me. I did have a fireman saying into the darkness, "Come toward the light." I believe that I did have angels encamped around our house, protecting both me and my precious newborn from serious harm.

God wants to walk with you through every moment of your life. You can be as close to Him as you want to be. He is available every moment of the day. He isn't too busy for you. He isn't bored with you. He isn't disgusted that you come back to Him again and again, just like Elizabeth and Zechariah did when they prayed for a child. God wants to be with you personally. He wants prayer to be as simple as breathing and as powerful as giving birth.

Learning to Respond to God Like Mary Did

We tend to make prayer too difficult and religious. We need to be more like Mary, who innocently trusted God to be true to His word. She wasn't cynical; she wasn't sarcastic; she wasn't angry. She was able to come to God uninhibited.

I am on this journey with you. I have neglected prayer and tried to "work my way" to the answer. I have been cynical, sarcastic, disappointed, and angry with God. My point is that all of us can learn to pray so heaven hears.

Just to be clear again, God is not up in heaven listening to your prayers with a scorecard. He is not comparing you to someone else. He is not waiting for you to follow some sort of legalistic secret code. Our main guide to learn about authentic, heartfelt prayer is the Bible. As we tell the story, remember Mary and the other characters in this book are real people with real problems.

The Key of Faith

Faith unlocks the door to prayer and opens the way to God's presence. It may seem simple, but it is truly profound. The way that you can have favor with God and please Him is through faith. If you want to learn about prayer, you have to have faith. You have to believe that God rewards those who diligently seek Him.[2] To be diligent is to actively pursue God. Your eager and earnest pursuit of God doesn't fade away in a day. You are persistent and tireless.

To be a woman of faith in prayer will require that you take risks. It's a walk of faith to constantly face unknowns. Obeying God does not guarantee that you will be free from disappointments or problems. When Mary said yes to God about being Jesus' mom, she didn't know the heartbreak she would experience when she watched Him being crucified on the cross. Our walk of faith will not be free from pain and loss, but it will be filled with God's presence as He leads us every step of the way. Prayer is communing with the One who walks with us on our faith journey.

A Song of Prayer

I encourage you to speak (or sing) Mary's song of prayer out loud. Her prayer is known as the *Magnificat* and has been sung by the most famous choirs throughout the ages. The words of her prayer of praise are based on Scripture. In order for us to pray like Mary prayed, we need to form our prayers in agreement with the Word of God.

Mary responded,

> "Oh, how my soul praises the Lord.
> How my spirit rejoices in God my Savior!
> For he took notice of his lowly servant girl,
> and from now on all generations will call me blessed.
> For the Mighty One is holy,
> and he has done great things for me.
> He shows mercy from generation to generation
> to all who fear him.
> His mighty arm has done tremendous things!
> He has scattered the proud and haughty ones.
> He has brought down princes from their thrones
> and exalted the humble.
> He has filled the hungry with good things
> and sent the rich away with empty hands.
> He has helped his servant Israel
> and remembered to be merciful.
> For he made this promise to our ancestors,
> to Abraham and his children forever."

Luke 1:46–55

— 2 —
Learning to Pray
with Faith

Ready to begin a trust-walk, where you learn more about the power of faith in prayer? The first step is to establish a firm foundation—to understand what it means to pray as a woman walking in faith.

> And it is impossible to please God without faith. Anyone who wants to come to him must believe that God exists and that he rewards those who sincerely seek him.
>
> Hebrews 11:6

1. What is God saying to you in Hebrews 11:6?
2. What does God promise you in this verse?
3. What two things does God desire for you to believe?

Earnestly seeking God should be a lifetime goal for every believer. You may not *feel* persistent and tireless, but you are transformed in the process of praying through difficult situations. Fresh faith is required for each day.

4. Read Hebrews 11:1. What is God saying to you in this verse?

5. Reflect on Mary's situation. How did she find confidence in God even when what God promised her was difficult for her to understand?

6. Describe the transformation that happened in Mary from when the angel first appeared to her in Luke 1:29–31 to when she embraced God's will in Luke 1:38.

God calls each of us to walk by faith, not by sight. To truly walk in faith, you will need to take risks. As you enter into unchartered waters, you need to rely on God to lead and guide you. There are no perfect coordinates that protect you from the storms of life. As you grow, and have faith in God, you are able to calm the storms of your life like Jesus did.

Just because you obey God does not mean that it will be smooth sailing forever and ever. Obedience opens the door for God to help you. Obedience connects you with God's plan in the midst of the process of life. Prayer requires you and me to trust God.

Praying with Confidence, Boldness, and Grace

7. Take time to reflect on your last week. What situation in your life shakes your confidence?

8. Write down 2 Timothy 1:6 (NIV), and insert your name in the Scripture. Post this personalized version in a place where you will see it every day.

9. In chapter 1, you read about a very dark and desperate experience where God called me to come toward the light. In what situation in your life do you need to come toward the light? Write down a prayer to God where you ask for His light to lead you and guide you.

Replacing Fear with Faith

Fear puts God on trial. When we are fearful or anxious, we are declaring that we can't fully trust in God to care about the details of our lives.

The Lies of Fear

> I can't pray.
> God doesn't hear my prayers.
> God doesn't care.
> Nothing changes anyway.

The Truth of Faith

> I am a woman of faith.
> I will come toward His light.
> I will seek God diligently.
> God rewards me with His favor.
> I am confident that He will hear me.
> My prayers move mountains.
> God answers my prayers.
> I trust God.
> I will walk in faith.

Increasing Your Passion

Your passion for God will increase as you activate your faith. Take this action step this week.

10. This week, activate your faith by praying out loud for someone in need. It may be someone that you know and love or it

could be a person you just met. Trust God that He will set up a divine appointment for you to pray for someone. Write down the name of the person you prayed for and how it felt to activate this area of your prayer life.

Extending God's Grace

A great way to grow in your prayer life is to gather a group of women to study and pray together. Just as you need God's grace to become a woman who moves mountains, you can extend His grace to others. Your prayer life will be multiplied when you agree with others in prayer.

For Group Discussion

Bonus Video: Have you ever felt desperate for help? I sure have. Watch the bonus video on transforming fear into faith at www. SueDetweiler.com, and see how God works in our lives when it feels like we are alone and our hope is all but gone.

11. Describe a desperate time in your life when you cried out to God for help. How did He answer your prayer? What do you hope to gain from this study of *Women Who Move Mountains: Praying with Confidence, Boldness, and Grace*?

Bonus Journal Pages: Download chapter 2 journal pages at www.Sue Detweiler.com.

3

I Am Chosen

Transforming Rejection into Calling

"Walking back into a church after so many years of being turned off by hypocrisy was really tough. I was terrified. I didn't know how to be around church people. But I needed to go in headfirst. I knew that my life was about to change and it had to. Our marriage was at a breaking point. I was in my early thirties, but I felt like I was a little girl again."

As my friend Marti Martin told me her story, my heart broke for this little girl. Now Marti is an author who goes into maximum security prisons to help rehabilitate sex offenders.

"My father was a convicted rapist. My mom had to raise us alone. She would say, 'I wish you weren't born. I wish you would die.' She went from crisis to crisis. She beat me, and then her husbands and lovers molested me.

"I wanted to go to church when I was a little girl. My clothes were ratty, and I wanted to look nice. One time, when I was invited, I looked down at my dirty shoes and said, 'I can't go.' The kind woman persisted, 'If I held you the whole time would you go with me?' I nodded. She picked me up, wearing her matching pink outfit and pink purse. But the church people disappointed me with their broken promises and hypocrisy.

"Now as a grown woman, I knew I didn't have a choice. My husband, Stan, sat me down after only three months of marriage and said, 'I love you but I can't stay married to you.' I knew immediately what he was talking about. I was unpleasable. He couldn't do anything up to my standard. I was constantly negative and critical.

"I loved Stan. I didn't want to lose him. So I swallowed my fear. I had already been at church for about a year, but now I knew that I had to go deeper with God. My marriage depended on it. Self-confrontation is a difficult thing to do. It was easy for me to confront people with *their* flaws, but now I had to confront mine. 'God, go ahead and shake up everything in my life,' I cried.

"During prayer, I felt God wanted to reveal himself to me as my Father. I had to learn to know God as my daddy and truly learn to forgive all those who hurt me. I had to spend time in prayer every day just to be nice. I needed to be in God's presence to find God's heart and gain His perspective. I tend to have quick negative reactions because of past pain. God uses prayer to cleanse and heal me of my wounds.

"In prayer, I begged God to give me a mentor who would love me and pour into my life. He answered my prayer with 'No, I'm going to make you into a woman who is an example to others.'

"I had no idea at that point that God would take me to the prisons to speak with convicted rapists, molesters, and pedophiles. The first time I spoke I was terrified. These fifty men walked in looking both normal and scary. I thought of all the stories of all the people they had hurt. My voice trembled as I looked them in the eyes.

"Behaviorism will not cure sex offenders. I knew they needed the same power of God that had freed me."

Abandonment Traumatizes the Soul

How old were you when you realized that the world can be vicious? What prompted you to feel inferior or left out for the first time? Were you the last one chosen for the team? Did someone make fun of the way you looked? Or maybe it was because of the color of your skin. Did your mom abandon you? Did your dad abuse you? Did someone steal your innocence before you knew what innocence was?

If our childhood wounds are not healed, we simply carry them into adulthood. Oh, we learn how to survive. Women learn how to dress up and hide imperfections. But the stabbing pains of rejection remain; they go deeper. Rejection scars the essence of who we are and who we hope to become. It creates an emptiness in our hearts and souls.

Rejection can make you feel like something is wrong with you. It's difficult to pray with conviction when the Enemy's oppressive cloud hangs over your head.

We live on an orphan planet, where so many of us have been abandoned and have deeply wounded hearts. Hurt people hurt other people. Rejected people reject other people. If you and I are not healed of the orphan mentality of this present age, we will carry it into our homes and families and into our futures. This orphan mindset hinders our prayer life with emotional stress and angst. But everyone who comes to faith in Jesus Christ is adopted as a son or daughter:

> So you have not received a spirit that makes you fearful slaves. Instead, you received God's Spirit when he adopted you as his own children. Now we call him, "Abba, Father." For his Spirit joins with our spirit to affirm that we are God's children.
>
> Romans 8:15–16

The mentality of an orphan is based on the fear that our needs will not get met. We become slaves to this fear and rejection, acting out our hurt and wounding through self-protection. Unhealed, this toxic thinking leads to a swamp of demonic activity.

41

Have you ever spent time in prayer and left your quiet time depressed or anxious? Rejection is a trap from Satan that will keep you away from fulfilling, joy-filled times of prayer.

You and I have been called to an intimate relationship with the God of the universe! We discover the depths of this love relationship through heartfelt prayer. Confusion surrounding your call to this intimate relationship can paralyze your prayer life.

The light of God's love and redemption breaks through this murky fog of rejection and abandonment to offer us hope. God not only values and esteems each one of His creations, but He has adopted us: "Even before he made the world, God loved us and chose us in Christ to be holy and without fault in his eyes" (Ephesians 1:4).

A key to overcoming rejection is found through intimacy with the Father. Embracing our acceptance and call from the Father requires focused meditation on God's truth to force out the lies of abandonment.

Being Rejected for Who You Are

When we were out taking pictures with an old camera and a timer, Wayne said, "Sue, I see God's gift and calling on your life. I will do everything I can to release you into the ministry that you are called to." He said those words and the camera's slow shutter snapped. I've treasured that picture. When the picture was developed, we were surprised that the light had created a rainbow effect over Wayne and me as we looked at each other. The rainbow made me think of God's promise to us as a couple and Wayne's promise to me.

However, as a woman who grew up in a Mennonite community, the thought that a woman could be released into ministry was a pioneering idea. For me, to accept God's call to serve in pastoral ministry meant that I would be rejected and misunderstood by those who did not agree with our convictions. I struggled with my own insecurity over God's call on my life.

It was nearly seven years after my husband and I began our ministry together when I finally had a measure of breakthrough over my fear of rejection. I reached out to a neighbor who loved God with her whole heart. Her husband traveled in music ministry. With my baby in a stroller, I went to her home to see if she would like to begin a prayer group together for our neighborhood.

She looked at me like she had been waiting for this opportunity to attack my role as a woman pastor. "How can you expect me to come into agreement in prayer when I don't agree with who you are and what you are doing? How can you be a good mother to your children and a good homemaker if you are a woman in ministry?"

I was blindsided by her response, and the blood drained from my face. Honestly, I don't remember how I escaped the conversation and made it out the door. My knuckles were white as I pushed the stroller home. My lips were quivering. I burst into the house with my daughter on my hip, practically throwing her into Wayne's arms. I collapsed into sobs.

Through the blubbering, my husband was able to piece together the same old struggle of whether or not God had called me. This was not a new topic for us. Wayne had listened over and over to my internal struggle of being a woman in ministry. Here I was again, a puddle of tears at my husband's feet.

With the baby on one hip and his hand on the other, he firmly said, "Sue, get up! *You know* this is a lie from the Enemy. *You know* that this is an attack. *You know* that you are called! Get up!"

You might be thinking he lacked compassion. No. My husband was my hero that day. He stirred me to faith in God's call on my life. It was the most validating thing he could say.

Wayne is a man of God. He hears His voice. God knew that I needed not only to hear my calling from Him, I needed to hear His voice through my husband—He created us to be one.

Through years of prayer and study, I felt a calm peace and a faith that God had indeed called me, and my fear fled. I knew that many would not agree with the convictions of my heart, but that was okay.

I took a giant leap forward in faith as I shut the door to fear. I became increasingly confident. I became less controlled by people's opinions of me. Nor did I feel like I needed to convince them of my own convictions. The Spirit of God speaks to our hearts. We must continue to agree on what is the most important: Jesus Christ is Savior, Lord, Redeemer, and Healer.

I didn't have women in ministry as role models growing up in my Mennonite community. I really had no idea how much of a pioneer I was called to be. My husband and I felt called to minister side by side. We were both ordained on the same day.

At our ordination service, my father shared an emotion-filled testimony of God's call on my life from the time I was in my mother's womb. My father had been in Bible college, married to my mom, and talking about going to Brazil as a missionary. They already had three young sons and were living in a tiny trailer when my mom became pregnant with me. As he struggled over his calling, Dad chose to stay in the States and raise his family. My mom was heartbroken. She had felt a call as a missionary and hoped that Dad would answer the call as well. She felt like it was her fault. So she began to cry out to God that the child in her womb would fulfill her call to the nations. She claimed Jeremiah 1 for my life:

> The Lord gave me this message: "I knew you before I formed you in your mother's womb. Before you were born I set you apart and appointed you as my prophet to the nations."
>
> Jeremiah 1:4–5

As Dad passionately shared this message at my ordination service, we sensed God's call and affirmation. My Father in heaven, my dad, and my husband all affirmed and encouraged me to step out and lead.

You have been made unique with a calling from God to stand out in certain areas of your life. Yet it is often in the areas of calling that you will experience the most rejection. When that happens, we are in danger of rejecting our calling through doubt.

Barren and "Cursed by God"

Have you ever noticed that it is often the women who wanted to have children all of their lives who seem to struggle with infertility? They feel called to have a child, but their efforts are spurned. Many lessons are learned from women in the Bible who struggled to have children.

Hannah battled rejection as she waited on God to fulfill her calling. What the Bible calls barrenness was seen as a curse, and with it came rejection. Imagine how Hannah felt as you read her story.

Elkanah had two wives, Hannah and Peninnah. Peninnah had children, but Hannah did not. Each year Elkanah would travel to Shiloh to worship and sacrifice to the Lord of Heaven's Armies at the Tabernacle. The priests of the Lord at that time were the two sons of Eli—Hophni and Phinehas. On the days Elkanah presented his sacrifice, he would give portions of the meat to Peninnah and each of her children. And though he loved Hannah, he would give her only one choice portion because the Lord had given her no children. So Peninnah would taunt Hannah and make fun of her because the Lord had kept her from having children. Year after year it was the same—Peninnah would taunt Hannah as they went to the Tabernacle. Each time, Hannah would be reduced to tears and would not even eat.

"Why are you crying, Hannah?" Elkanah would ask. "Why aren't you eating? Why be downhearted just because you have no children? You have me—isn't that better than having ten sons?"

1 Samuel 1:2–8

Imagine the painful taunting of a rival wife who blames your infertility on God's curse. Hannah's lack was magnified by her rival's abundant fertility. If that wasn't bad enough, her husband was married to this woman—and it was legal!

The rejection Hannah felt whenever her husband lay in Peninnah's arms must have been immense. They didn't have thick walls or closed doors to muffle the sound of their intimacy. They slept in tents. It wasn't difficult for Hannah to know when her husband slept with the other woman. She could count the weeks from the time they had intercourse and see Peninnah's body change shape as she carried a baby.

Rejection and jealousy must have clawed deep into Hannah's spirit. Even though he said he loved her, she must have felt abandoned by her husband. Spurned by her rival and mocked by Peninnah's fertility, Hannah could have felt abandoned by God himself.

Abandoned by God

Most women wonder at some point: *How could God allow this to happen to me?* In your mind you may know that God would never abandon you. Yet why is it that at times you feel disappointed that God didn't come through for you?

You may long to be married. You have grown older and your chances seem slimmer. Where is God? You know that Scripture tells you that God doesn't disappoint. Yet you feel disappointed.

Maybe you married early, but now you feel stuck. The man you married is a workaholic, or he is addicted to pornography, or sleeping with other women. You feel spurned by your own husband. *God, where are you? Don't you care?*

You may have gone through a divorce you didn't want and feel beaten down by the rejection.

You may have been abused as a child. The father who should have protected you became a predator in your bed. *God, why didn't you protect me? Where were you when I was being abused?*

Hope fades. Dreams die.

Desperation Is a Driving Force in Prayer

Hannah was desperate. When she faced her trial of infertility, she didn't have anyone to help her carry the burden except God. Hannah's husband, Elkanah, had given her a choice portion to make an offering to God when they went to Shiloh once a year. He really didn't understand what the big deal was.

Every husband wants to be first to his wife. Of course, Elkanah was living a double standard. He wanted to be the most important to Hannah, but he still embraced the second wife like every wealthy man in his culture did at the time. Hannah felt all alone. I'm sure you can empathize with the desperation of her story:

> And she was in bitterness of soul, and prayed to the Lord and wept in anguish. Then she made a vow and said, "O Lord of hosts, if You will indeed look on the affliction of Your maidservant and remember me . . ."
>
> 1 Samuel 1:10–11 NKJV

Have you ever focused your desperation like an arrow that hits the target in prayer to God? People do a lot of crazy things when they are desperate. They can become violent and impulsive. Sometimes they give up and try to medicate the bitterness in their soul with alcohol or their drug of choice. But sometimes that desperation can lead us to the feet of God.

Hannah is crying out to God and asking Him to remember her. She is dealing with her own feelings of rejection and holding her need up to God. She is trusting that God is good. She is willing to lay it all on the line for God. Yes, Hannah is asking for a son. But she also offers to give that son back to God: "If you will look upon my sorrow and answer my prayer and give me a son, then I will give him back to you. He will be yours for his entire lifetime" (1 Samuel 1:11).

Her request for the gift of this destined child is not a selfish request. She wants what God wants. Is there a prayer deep in your heart that you are holding back because you think it is self-centered? Dare to pray the deepest desires of your heart. Dare to dream about the things that seem impossible to you. Nothing is impossible for God.

47

If it is truly God's will for your life, it will be about much more than just you. You will find the joy of fulfillment, but your destiny is about serving God and others.

God Uses the Weight of Your Heart

God uses the heaviness of your heart to meet your needs. He joins them with the burden of His own heart. During the same time that Hannah was infertile, the nation of Israel was unfruitful as well. Imagine the burden of God's heart for the spiritual needs of His people.

Hannah was praying about her own specific need, but God saw the larger picture. He heard Hannah's cry and He answered with what became a turning point in history. The nation of Israel had degenerated both morally and politically. The priesthood was corrupt. In fact, the priest Eli's own sons were sleeping with women who came to the temple to pray. It was a season of deep spiritual need.

Before the foundation of time, God dreamed about Samuel. God destined Samuel to be a voice to speak on His behalf to the people. Hannah probably had no idea that her intense intercession was motivated partly by her own desire, but largely because of God's historical purpose.

You and I have been chosen by God to be His hands in history. *You* have been chosen for greatness. God picked *you* to be a historymaker. You and I won't be able to see the whole picture like God does. We simply agree with God in prayer for His will to be done. We choose to be chosen.

Hannah was birthing in prayer a son who would be a blessing to the whole nation. She gave God the longings of her heart. He moved on her behalf and advanced His purpose at the same time.

God moves through people who pray. He places burdens on our hearts that can only be satisfied when fully surrendered to God. Our faith-filled desperation gives way to purpose-driven lives that impact nations.

Why then are we so unaccustomed to seeing someone pour out their heart to God unreservedly? Eli himself was so unfamiliar with seeing someone pray to God with desperation that he assumed Hannah must be drunk. Hannah answered Eli, saying, "No, my lord, I am a woman of sorrowful spirit. I have drunk neither wine nor intoxicating drink, but have poured out my soul before the Lord" (1 Samuel 1:15 NKJV).

Prayer Is Pouring Your Heart Out to God

Prayer is as natural as breathing. Prayer should not be restricted to certain times of the day or week when we have a quiet time. Prayer is living and active. Prayer is not perfectly contained in a checklist.

Prayer is not "doing our religious duty." We are called to pray big, risky prayers that require an answer from the One who is more powerful than anyone in the universe.

Most important, prayer is about knowing God intimately. It is about struggling to give birth to God's purposes. And it is about embracing the sweet presence of God and allowing the wind of His Spirit to blow freely.

Prayer Is a Powerful Weapon

Prayer is a powerful defense against the forces of evil when wielded in the hands of a life-giving woman of prayer. When you join yourself to God's purposes, you will be for life and against death. The prayers you pray today will outlast your life here on earth. The prayers that you pray in agreement with God's will continue long after you are gone.

When Hannah prayed, she was a barren woman crying out to God for a son. Her prayers birthed a new season for a nation. Samuel was raised up in the transitional time of Israel. Samuel grew into a priest, a prophet, and a judge who led his nation.

Prayer Launches Destiny

Hannah was chosen and destined to be a mother. Even when others didn't believe, she believed God. She trusted God. She surrendered to God. You and I are chosen for specific purposes. It is prayer that enables us to find and fulfill God's purpose.

Hannah overcame her feelings of rejection and embraced the power of her calling. She birthed her destiny through prayer. She overcame her rejection and the mockery of her rival by falling on her knees before God.

Throw off rejection with the power of your calling to pray. Before you look down the line and assume that Hannah was some spiritual giant who knew how to really pray, embrace the fact that you are called to pray.

Yes, you have been called to pray. When I was a young woman, I didn't see myself as having a calling to pray. If I had an urgent need, I would call my mom to pray for me. *She* had a calling to pray. I still share my prayer requests with my mom and other people who I know will pray. Yet power and peace come as I embrace *my* call to pray.

Making Powerful Prayer Simple

Here are a few simple ways of thinking about prayer.

PRAYER IS CONVERSATION

Prayer is talking to God and listening for the ways that He talks to you. He can talk to you as you read Scripture. He can talk to you as you watch the sunrise. He can talk to you when you tuck your children into bed. Talk to God. Listen for God.

PRAYER IS BEING REAL

Prayer is transparently coming to God with your stuff. It's not so much a complaining session about everything that is wrong. Think of it as a spiritual chiropractic adjustment. One thing that I have begun doing whenever I feel anxious, sad, or rejected is going to the Word. I begin to read the Word, often the Psalms, until I find a promise from God that addresses my situation. I then pray and declare God's promises over my life.

PRAYER IS RELATIONSHIP

Prayer is not something you do in the morning and then forget about during the rest of the day. Prayer is walking with Jesus step by step. Prayer is allowing the Holy Spirit into your daily life. Prayer is crawling into the Father's lap when you are afraid.

PRAYER NEVER ENDS

If you have ever felt like your prayers were bouncing off the ceiling and coming back to you unanswered, then you are experiencing the spiritual static caused by this world. Prayer is not something that ends with this lifetime. Prayer is something that continues into the next life. If you have received Jesus Christ as your Lord and Savior, your conversation with Him in this world is just a warm-up for the next.

PRAYER IS AN EXERCISE IN FAITH

Faith is what moves mountains. To have faith is to begin to see what God sees. To have faith is to hear His voice and act on it. You have the power to choose what God chooses. You have been invited to walk with the God of the universe to make history happen.

YOU ARE CHOSEN TO PRAY

You have been chosen by God to pray. Your prayer life is not like anyone else's on the planet. You have been chosen by God to walk with Him and talk with Him. Your prayers will be simple yet profound. God hears your prayer. Your prayers have the power to change history.

∽PRAYER∽
for Transforming Rejection
into Calling

Everlasting God and Father, I am your daughter. I have been cho-sen by you, anointed by you, appointed by you, to fulfill my own unique destiny. Thank you for holding the whole world in your hands. I pour out my heart to you. In my own desperation, I trust you to make me a historymaker. Use my prayers to impact history. Use my prayers to launch destiny. Use my prayers to bring to birth your purposes. I trust you, Father. I'm your daughter. I love you fully and completely. I rest my head on your shoulders. I embrace my calling. I am yours. Amen.

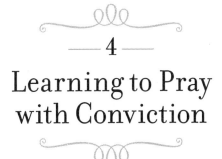

4

Learning to Pray
with Conviction

As we look at how to replace rejection with calling, let's study how Jesus walked free from rejection in His life. Jesus is our model for how to pray.

1. Read Luke 3:21–22. How was Jesus' calling announced?

2. What is God saying to you in this verse about your calling?

3. Read Luke 4:1–4. How was Jesus' call as God's "dearly loved Son" challenged by the devil?

4. Why did the Holy Spirit drive Jesus into the wilderness?

5. Read Luke 4:14–15. How did Jesus enter public ministry?

6. Read Luke 4:16–21. What is significant about the words in the scroll that Jesus read?

7. Read Luke 4:22. How did the people of Nazareth first respond to Jesus?

8. Read Luke 4:23–30. What is God saying to you in these verses?

9. How did Jesus deal with rejection in his own life?

Learning to Pray with Conviction

Jesus is our hero who shows us how to replace rejection with calling. God had given Jesus the promise that He was His "dearly beloved Son." The devil tempted Jesus to doubt His calling by saying in essence, "If you are the Son of God, prove yourself." Jesus did not back down in fear and give any power to the Enemy's attack. He overcame the devil and moved into public ministry with power and anointing. He faced His first rejection from His hometown of Nazareth. Rather than try to obtain the people's favor, He challenged their unbelief. Their rejection was so strong that they wanted to kill Him right there at the edge of the cliff.

10. Read Luke 4:31–37. Does the Scripture show Jesus spending time overcoming wounds of rejection from His hometown?

11. With Jesus as your example, compare how you deal with rejection. Are you able to move right into your called assignment, or do you lose time trying to "fix" the rejection you are experiencing?

12. Reflect honestly on your prayer life. When you have been rejected, do you get stuck praying about how you feel about the situation and asking God how to fix it? If so, how is God leading you to pray in the future? If not, what has been the secret of your prayer life?

You and I face a very real enemy who tries to keep us off balance. All power and authority belongs to Jesus, who has called us. When Jesus called you, He shared His power and authority with you. The Spirit will only lead you into conflicts that you are equipped and anointed by Him to win. It's time that we shut the door on the Enemy, who is trying to use our emotions and weakness to accuse us.

If you are making a difference and advancing God's kingdom, like Jesus, you will experience rejection. That doesn't mean that we should move forward obnoxiously, lacking people skills or tact. Yet we need to be able to rest in the fact that our acceptance and value from God are not based on our performance but on grace. We all make mistakes. In other words, we all sin and fall short of God's best (Romans 3:23).

13. Read 1 John 1:9. What does the Word call us to do when we make mistakes?

14. What promise from God do you find in 1 John 1:9?

The devil often uses the oppressive cloud of condemnation to keep you from praying with conviction. The Enemy's trap attacks the essence of who you are. The Enemy tries to separate you from God and stall your prayer life.

The Holy Spirit, on the other hand, will convict you of sin like a ray of sunlight bursting through a cloud. We are called to "confess our sins to him, [and if we do] he is faithful and just to forgive us our sins and to cleanse us from all wickedness" (1 John 1:9). Repentance is a wonderful gift that helps reconcile us to God. You are able to pray with increased conviction when there is no known sin in your life.

15. Take a moment to allow the Holy Spirit to search your life. Is there anything hindering you from having a clean conscience before God? Simply listen to God's voice and write down what He says.

Sometimes the sin that is creating distance between you and God in prayer is sin that someone else has committed against you. We are to aggressively deal with any seed of bitterness in our hearts through the power of forgiveness.

16. Read Colossians 3:12–14. What does this passage of Scripture reveal about God's calling in your life?

17. What does Colossians 3:12–14 say about forgiveness?

18. Ask the Holy Spirit to reveal to you anyone you need to forgive. Write down the name or names the Holy Spirit brings to mind.

Take time to forgive from your heart each one that you have listed. If the pain is deep, set up a time with a spiritual leader in your life to help you pray a prayer of forgiveness and to receive God's healing and grace.

Praying with Confidence, Boldness, and Grace

19. Take time to reflect on the last month. Is there a situation in your life where you have felt rejected?
20. How has the Enemy tried to shake your confidence by questioning your calling and identity?
21. Take time to listen to God's voice and write down what He is saying to you personally about your calling.

Replacing Rejection with Calling

Rejection gives power to the Enemy.

When we allow feelings of rejection to take root in our hearts, we are opening the door to the Enemy to accuse our identity and distract us from our calling.

The Lies of Rejection

There is something wrong with me.
I need to fix this so other people will like me.
Maybe God has not called me.
I am all alone.

The Truth of Calling

I am chosen.

I am a joy and delight to my heavenly Father.

I am adopted as His heir.

I am the apple of His eye.

In my weakness God is strong.

I can do all things through Christ
who strengthens me.

Increasing Your Passion

Your passion will increase as you embrace your unique calling. Take this action step this week:

22. Activate your faith by writing out your vision statement. Include Scriptures that identify your calling. You already read Jesus' mission statement from Luke 4:18–19. Your personal mission statement will include your core values, purpose, and call. Go to www.SueDetweiler.com for an example and a free vision statement form to download.

Extending God's Grace

There is power in united prayer to break the Enemy's attack on our lives. When we pray for one another's weaknesses and call on God's grace, powerful change happens within each of us.

For Group Discussion

Bonus Video: Have you ever been so embarrassed you wanted to disappear? Embarrassment feels like rejection. Watch the bonus

video on transforming rejection into calling at www.SueDetweiler
.com as we learn to discern our calling from our failures.

23. Describe a time in your life when you experienced rejection.
    How did God help to comfort and heal your soul? Did you
    get stuck, or did you find God's grace to move forward in
    your calling? In what ways can we pray for you right now?

Bonus Journal Pages: Download chapter 4 journal pages at www.
SueDetweiler.com.

5

I Am Healed

Transforming Brokenness into Wholeness

"As a kid," Lori explained, "I just wanted someone to love me for who I am."

Lori lived with her single mom and younger sister. "Our home was filled with her boyfriends and husbands and instability. I was four when I was first sexually abused by one of the friends that Mom left me with. I was exposed to pornography and forced to act things out.

"I didn't have a safe place. I spent most of my childhood trying to protect my younger sister or my mom. It was horrifying watching my mom being beaten and fearing for our lives.

"My mom left me with a Catholic family for a year and a half. In church, they showed us pictures of priests and nuns who had been martyred. I saw the images of these martyred saints and thought, *That is how I feel.*

"When I was eleven, I opened up to a nun and shared how I had been sexually abused as a child. She called the priest. Then the priest called the family I was living with, who also called my mom. I told them my whole story—and nothing happened. My mom convinced them that I was lying. The priest left and told me not to lie again. I knew the priest was my channel to God. When the priest rejected me, I felt abandoned by God himself.

"I could no longer live with the Catholic family, and my mom didn't want me because I was so 'bad.' I thought something must be horribly wrong with me. I began to run away, steal things, and act out of my wounding. My mom called my father, whom I had never met, and told him I had to live with him when I was twelve.

"One day my dad and stepmom picked me up for dinner. Then they took me home to live with them. Whenever I tried to talk about things that had happened to me, my dad would say, 'That's your old life; never speak of it again.' They were overly strict with me, but it gave me structure.

"I grew up in their home with all my emotions bottled up. When I met my husband, I fell in love with him because he was safe. I knew he wouldn't hurt me. We were fine until I became pregnant. It triggered my fear of becoming a mother. It was eight years into my marriage and I freaked out. Later I was able to meet their physical needs, but I couldn't connect emotionally with my husband or my kids.

"My husband and I were having trouble with communication. One day I woke up and said, 'We should go to church to get help.'

"We didn't realize that it was God himself that we needed. We went to church to get help, but it all blew up in our faces. I ended up being manipulated and controlled in a toxic relationship with a church member. After a year, we had a short-lived sexual affair. He knew I was wounded and he was using me. I knew he was manipulating me, but I still said yes.

"It was a common theme in my life: thinking that I was going to God for help and getting into a huge mess because of people. I had dreams that I was hanging over a pit by one hand. It was terrifying. I would look up and my hand would disappear into the light.

"My husband and I were both devastated. I left the adulterous relationship. We stayed in church and tried to heal. We were in so much pain we didn't know what to do.

"I finally surrendered my life to Jesus because I was so hurt. We entered into counseling, and I opened up my emotions. It was the first time my husband heard all the details of what I had gone through.

"A defining moment in my healing process was learning how to listen to God in prayer. I learned to sit and be silent before God and listen for His voice. It was there that I allowed all the memories of what had happened to come to the surface. I spent nine months identifying all the lies that I believed about God and replacing them with the truth of His Word.

"I hadn't cried over my childhood before, and I sobbed before God. I felt angry and abandoned and left alone in these situations. It was through prayer that I found healing. Without prayer, there is no way to be grounded in the truth about God.

"Without prayer, I didn't have a compass for my life. I spent most of my life just reacting. There are things that happen in life to this day, and all I can do is pray. I can't fix it. I can't change it. But I can pray. We have to pray with a surrendered heart. That's when we find His healing.

"Early on in my prayer life, I spent time asking God to take the pain away. Now I spend more time meditating on God's Word and praying for His truth. God is not my Mr. Fix It Band-Aid Dude. God is my Father. He can take all the stuff in my life, and He pours back His unconditional love. Now my prayers are motivated by awe and reverence for who He is."

The Silent Prayers of the Walking Wounded

When you feel broken inside, how do you pray? If, like Lori, you have been abused, you may find it difficult to come into God's presence. If you were wounded at your father's hand, you may have difficulty praying to your Father in heaven.

If you live and breathe on planet earth, you have been scarred by life. You may not have suffered sexual abuse, but at some point in your life your identity has been assaulted. And you may have moments—or years—where you are tempted to *blame* it on God rather than *turn* to God.

The Enemy of your soul has a plan for your life. Your adversary sets up bad situations and then blames God for them. Part of the assault is to keep you from turning to God as your only source of hope.

Demonic forces set up recurring situations in your life that make you feel like something is wrong with you. On the outside you may look fine, but every once in a while something touches that wounded place and you sense the deeper emptiness.

It's in this moment that you have a choice. Will you fill that emptiness with some sort of addiction to medicate your pain? Or will you in your desperation turn to God as your healer?

A Desperate Woman Reflects on Who Jesus Is

She was marked. Everyone knew her as a sinner. Her reputation was ruined. Her identity soiled. Who could she turn to? She carried an alabaster flask [1] (Luke 7:36–50). It carried the precious fragrant oil that was meant for her dowry.

This woman had the audacity to show up uninvited to the garden party of a Pharisee. She felt safe with Jesus. Maybe she had been in the crowd when Jesus cried out, "Come to me, all of you who are weary and carry heavy burdens, and I will give you rest" (Matthew 11:28).

She was tired. She was weary. She had lost hope. There was no place for her to rest because her soul was tormented. She was hanging on to a rope that didn't reach the ground. She couldn't go home. She couldn't go to the temple. She was an immoral woman, in danger of being stoned to death for her sins. She thought long and hard about who Jesus was before she decided to take a risk.

Jesus was a different sort of man. He didn't look at women with lust in his eyes. Nor did He look at them with condemnation. His eyes were filled with perceptive hope. It was like He could see a person's past and future at the same time.

There were many rabbis who taught their male disciples that they were superior to women. A standard prayer was "Blessed are you, Lord, our God, ruler of the universe, who has not created me a woman."[2]

But Jesus didn't treat women like He was superior. He didn't treat them like they were cursed to forever be inferior. Jesus had a different way of relating to women. He treated them like they were human beings with intelligence and dignity.

As the desperate woman reflected on who Jesus was hope began to stir in her heart. Maybe with Jesus she had a chance for a new beginning. At any rate, it was worth the risk. As she thought about the most precious thing she had, she knew it was the alabaster jar that was her dowry.

Tears came to her eyes as she thought about her lost innocence. No one would marry her now. This alabaster flask was the sweetest thing she owned. She hung on to it as though it represented the pureness of who she was before she fell into sin.

A Desperate Woman Takes Action

She grabbed her alabaster jar and went to the garden where Simon the Pharisee was entertaining Jesus. Others were in the courtyard too, silently listening, cupping their ears to catch the conversation.

She wasn't able to hear everything they said, but she could capture Simon's rudeness to Jesus. When Jesus arrived, Simon didn't even tell a servant to wash Jesus' feet. He didn't greet Him with a kiss or anoint His head with oil. It was clear what Simon's motives were: to exalt himself by neglecting these customary gestures, which amounted to a put-down.

She felt a boldness come on her as the conversation slowed. Silently she came behind Jesus where he lounged on pillows. She couldn't hold back her emotions any longer. She had seen the woman who was healed of her bleeding and restored to wholeness. In every situation, Jesus met women with mercy, not condemnation.

As she knelt down behind Jesus, He turned and looked at her. Love, forgiveness, mercy, and honor flowed through His gaze. She was truly in God's presence, and she began to weep. Her tears washed Jesus' soiled feet. She let down her hair. Yes, she knew that should be reserved for her husband, but truly there was no one who had shown her that much love and gentleness. She took her hair in her hands and she began to dry Jesus' feet.

Then with love in her eyes and devotion in her heart, the woman broke open the alabaster flask. The fragrant oil flowed forth, a symbol of her love for Jesus. She was willing to sacrifice it all to anoint Him. He was the anointed One.

To Pray Effectively We Need to See Jesus for Who He Is

The woman with the alabaster flask was able to act boldly and transparently because of what she believed about Jesus. She believed that Jesus would receive her. She believed she was safe. She believed He would show both mercy and truth. She understood Jesus' heart because she had watched His actions.

Our prayer life needs to be undergirded by our biblical knowledge of who Jesus is. If we know that He is safe, we are more likely to run to Him than to an addiction or some other source to comfort ourselves.

To know Jesus intimately, we need to spend time with Him every day. I have grown from reading through the Bible every year, taking a section each day to get to know Him better. If we take time to journal what God is saying to us, we are able to go back and remember His words and apply them anew. Memorizing Scripture makes the Word ours. All of these spiritual disciplines help us grow closer to Jesus.

When we see Jesus for who He is—gentle, loving, merciful, longing to make us whole—we are emboldened to come to Him humbly. We don't try to hide our brokenness or cower in shame. Instead, we boldly bring our wounds to Him in order to be healed. His truth sets us free.

Don't Be a Pharisee

This garden party of Simon's took a definite turn when the immoral woman showed up—but not everyone was able to recognize it. Simon could have seen the beauty of God's mercy being actively demonstrated through Jesus. Instead, he was blinded by his own judgment.

A Pharisee in the days of Jesus was a set-apart follower of God. They were the ones who were devoted to God's Word and living it out in their daily lives. But they turned the law into ritualistic rules that made it impossible for real people to have a vibrant relationship with God.

I'm sorry to say that I spent many years of my life as a Pharisee. I had my own check boxes that I marked every day as I read God's Word and studied it. I got up early in the morning to pray. I fasted. I didn't think I was a Pharisee. That's the problem with spiritual pride—it blinds you.

Jesus warned, "Be on your guard against the yeast of the Pharisees, which is hypocrisy" (Luke 12:1 NIV).

Yeast is something that starts out very small, yet if you give it time and the right conditions it grows. Before you know it, you can be patting yourself on the back for "doing your duty" in prayer. Hypocrisy is living in pretense. It is pretending to have moral standards but missing the main point.

The main point about prayer is relationship, not ritual.

Don't miss the main point about prayer. Prayer is being real with God. Transparent. At times you may be unglued in your emotions and desperate in your need. At other times you may be quietly grateful.

Prayer is the beauty of being in God's presence without pretense.

Simon Missed the Main Point

Simon, the Pharisee who had invited Jesus to dinner, did not see the tenderness of the moment. Nor did he sense God's presence at work bringing healing and devotion. Instead, he became critical, saying to himself, "If this man were a prophet, he would know what kind of woman is touching him. She's a sinner!" (Luke 7:39).

When you get stuck in religiousness, you can think you are completely right about an issue and be totally on the opposite side of Jesus. In your religious pride, you can be like Simon and misjudge a person.

When you misjudge someone, imagine what your prayers are like. The worst thing about the blindness of a Pharisee is how much you can hurt others without intending to. Your intent can be to set things right. But because you are blinded by your own spiritual pride, you end up wounding others with your superior attitude.

Simon, blinded by his own pride, was channeling condemnation. Simon was not only judging the woman in his heart, but wrongly judging Jesus as well. Of course, he didn't say this out loud to Jesus, but Jesus answered his thoughts:

> "Simon," he said to the Pharisee, "I have something to say to you."
>
> "Go ahead, Teacher," Simon replied.
>
> Then Jesus told him this story: "A man loaned money to two people—500 pieces of silver to one and 50 pieces to the other. But neither of them could repay him, so he kindly forgave them both, canceling their debts. Who do you suppose loved him more after that?"
>
> Simon answered, "I suppose the one for whom he canceled the larger debt."
>
> "That's right," Jesus said.
>
> Luke 7:40–43

Notice how prim and proper Simon is acting. He calls Jesus "Teacher," which in Hebrew is *Rabboni*–where we get the word *rabbi.* He was using the term of honor for a Jewish scholar. The word literally means "master" or "great one."

> Then he turned to the woman and said to Simon, "Look at this woman kneeling here. When I entered your home, you didn't offer me water to wash the dust from my feet, but she has washed them with her tears and wiped them with her hair. You didn't greet me with a kiss, but from the time I first came in, she has not stopped kissing my feet. You neglected the courtesy of olive oil to anoint my head, but she has anointed my feet with rare perfume."
>
> Luke 7:44–46

Simon had come to Jesus in pride, and his own sin was publicly revealed. Simon's rudeness revealed his heart. Jesus went against the social culture of the day to confront religious pride. Jesus didn't stop there. Jesus was concerned about clarifying the new state of the woman's redemption publicly. He was confronting others' views of her as an "immoral" woman. He was restoring her innocence. Jesus said:

> "I tell you, her sins—and they are many—have been forgiven, so she has shown me much love. But a person who is forgiven little shows only little love." Then Jesus said to the woman, "Your sins are forgiven."
>
> The men at the table said among themselves, "Who is this man, that he goes around forgiving sins?"
>
> And Jesus said to the woman, "Your faith has saved you; go in peace."
>
> Luke 7:47–50

This radical encounter for the woman with the alabaster flask would not have happened unless she was willing to come close to Jesus. She came to Jesus broken, and she left healed and whole. Her sins were forgiven. She had come with faith and found salvation. She left the encounter blessed with peace.

Healing from Sexual Abuse

When was the first moment you realized something was broken in your life? I was sitting in health class when I heard the term *sexual abuse* for the first time. Just hearing it made me cringe. I had words for what happened to me.

I suddenly felt wounded on the inside. Unlike a china doll, which looks fragile on the outside, my broken places were hidden. On the outside I was a talented, straight-A student. I was a tennis and volleyball player, and a cheerleader who always had a smile on her face.

Sitting there in class, I felt dirty . . . ruined . . . soiled. My innocence was ransacked by the exploration of a selfish male. My mind began to think back to the different events that scarred me. I was only eight when I was broken on the inside. The twisted part of sexual abuse is that you sometimes love the person who hurt you. In a perverted way, you want to protect him from harm and exposure.

I was also confused. Was this the "right" way to act? A mixture of anger, dread, and shame swirled around the thoughts in my mind. It was like a hidden black hole was sucking me in.

In my own life, healing from sexual abuse has come gradually as I have brought my brokenness to Jesus to receive His healing. As I have sat with many women and heard their heartbreaking stories, mine would seem slight in comparison. I was never physically penetrated by the abuser, but I was violated. You and I don't have to compare our scars before coming to Jesus. He receives each one of us just as we are.

I first took my pain to a Christian counselor after I began having a series of dreams in college. These dreams revealed how hurt a little girl's heart can be when taken advantage of. As I began talking about the specifics of the abuse with the counselor, I realized how angry I was. Something had been stolen from me: my *innocence*.

At the Christian college I attended, there was a designated spot on campus with quiet rooms to pray. I began to take my Bible and journal there every day. Tears would silently fall down my cheeks as I got in touch with the pain.

I began to write my prayers to God. Then I would silently wait to see if I heard Him say anything back. I was amazed that when I listened, He responded. I filled my journal with healing words from Jesus. I encountered Jesus personally and His truth set me free (John 8:32).

Layer by layer my brokenness was replaced with His wholeness. These were some of the layers that I went through:

1. Acknowledging the pain.
2. Receiving Jesus' love and restored innocence.
3. Forgiving the one who abused me.
4. Setting up boundaries of safety.
5. Walking in wholeness.
6. Learning intimacy with my husband.
7. Raising children in an environment of safety.

Just when I thought the process was complete, I would go through a different stage in my life and find that I needed another layer of healing. I began to think of the process like peeling an onion. Every time the Holy Spirit peeled another layer back there were tears.

At every point of further healing in my life, I encountered Jesus in greater fullness. After being ministered to in prayer by others at a ministry event, I found myself worshiping Jesus with greater freedom. My heart was full of gratitude. I too had been forgiven much. My faith saved me. I could walk in peace and joy.

Healed

You can replace your brokenness with God's wholeness. Come to Him as you are. In your weakness, He will be your strength. Whatever you have done, or whatever has been done to you, you can bring it to Jesus. He knows. He cares. He heals. He delivers.

Whatever layer you are facing in your healing process, pray this prayer to Jesus.

∼PRAY∽

Jesus, thank you for restoring my stolen innocence. Sin scarred my soul, but your love makes me whole. Sin ransacked the essence of who I am, but you gave me a new identity. Sin stained me, marked me, rejected me, but you have received me. Jesus, in love and adoration I let my tears flow freely. I know you won't condemn me. You gave your precious blood to redeem me from the sin to cleanse me from my guilt and shame. Jesus, I am free in you. My heart has been made new. Thank you. Amen.

—6—
Learning to Pray
Healing Prayers

Learning to replace brokenness with wholeness is a process. We start out feeling weak, and step by step we learn to be empowered by His presence.

1. Read Isaiah 42:1–2. Who is the Lord's chosen servant in this passage?
2. Read Isaiah 42:3. How does the Lord treat the bruised?
3. Describe an area in your life that has been bruised or broken. This could be either from your childhood or adult years.
4. Read Isaiah 53:5. Describe the promise of healing in this passage.
5. Read Psalm 34:17–18. List the things that the Lord does for His people.
6. Read Psalm 103:1–6 out loud. List God's benefits.
7. How does the above passage speak to you about healing?
8. Read Luke 7:36–38. Why does the woman feel safe to approach Jesus in this intimate way?

9. Read Luke 7:47–50. What was Jesus' response to the woman?

10. Think about your own healing process. Is there a new layer of God's healing that you need? If so, write down the area. Acknowledge the pain and the sin of your situation.

11. Read Lamentations 3:23. What promise does God give in this Scripture passage?

12. Take a moment to listen to the Holy Spirit. Is there anyone in your life whom you need to forgive? If so, write down your forgiveness. As you write it down, let go of the pain.

13. Read Matthew 7:1–5. In what ways have you been tempted to fix others? As you find healing are you sometimes tempted to judge others who are struggling with sin?

Praying with Confidence, Boldness, and Grace

Often our minds gravitate toward areas in our lives where we need transformation. You and I can be tempted to struggle, strain, or strive to make things better. The Enemy loves to have you meditate on the negative rather than renew your mind with God's positive encouragement. Whatever you meditate on you will magnify.

14. Read Romans 12:1–2. According to this Scripture, how are you transformed?

15. Read and write down Philippians 4:19. What does this Scripture promise you?

16. Look through the Scriptures that you have read in this chapter. Choose at least one passage to write out and memorize. By meditating daily on God's Word, you will be transformed as you renew your mind.

17. Listen to God's voice. What steps is He calling you to take to cultivate an inner life of purity that manifests in a life of God's power flowing through your daily life?

Replacing Brokenness with Wholeness

Brokenness opens doors for the Enemy to attack you.

Our brokenness needs God's healing presence.

As we renew our minds, He transforms each of us from the inside out.

The Lies of Brokenness

If my outer environment would change,
my internal reality would be fine.

The way I am feeling is someone else's fault.

The Truth of Wholeness

I am a new creation in Christ.

My joy comes from God's presence.

He has already empowered me to be free from sin.

I can be close to God.

He is my healer.

Learning to Pray Healing Prayers

Jesus Christ was wounded for our sake. On the cross He bore our sin and shame. In this life we are wounded by the things that happen to us. In some ways, that wounding changes who we are. God's redemption takes the very areas where we have experienced the most pain and uses them to help heal others.

When Jesus was resurrected, He reached out His nail-scarred hands to His disciples. One way they recognized Him was by the scars He bore from His crucifixion—His suffering. God's redemptive healing in your life can take the areas of pain and loss and transform them to be a healing testimony to help others on their journey. As God brings healing to your life, He helps you to be a bridge of healing to others. He takes what the Enemy meant for evil and turns it into good. You may not feel like you have much of a testimony until you start to write out the simple ways that God has been faithful to you.

18. Write down your testimony of how God has healed you in the past and continues to heal you today. Be vulnerable and share your pain. Concentrate on the transformation that God has done and continues to do in your life. Share important Scriptures that have helped you on your healing journey. After you have written out your testimony, pray for an opportunity to share it with someone who needs encouragement. Remember to point to Jesus as the source of your healing.

Extending God's Grace

Like Lori, our brokenness can come from the hands of people in the church. You can begin to repair and heal by first trusting in God to lead you to other women who move mountains.

For Group Discussion

Bonus Video: We may see ourselves as broken. But others can see the light of hope in our weak areas. Watch this chapter's bonus video at www.SueDetweiler.com.

19. Describe the process of healing that you have gone through in your life. How did God empower you to walk in true freedom? Are there other areas in your life where you need a breakthrough? In what ways can we pray for you right now?

7

I Am Honored

Transforming Shame into Grace

Donna grew up with an awareness of shame. She was embarrassed that she was one of the poorest kids in town. She was known for blushing and hiding behind a bush when she was a teenager.

"One of my earliest memories was that of having to get up in the middle of the night to use the dirty outhouse. I was the youngest of nine and I refused to go out in the cold dark alone. It was a double-seater outhouse, and one of my six older sisters had to take me. We would sit there together. We had to use the pages of a Sears catalog to wipe with. We hated the colored pages because they were stiffer.

"I was so embarrassed about our outhouse because everyone else had indoor plumbing. When friends, even boyfriends, came to visit me, they had to use that old outhouse. It felt so dirty and old-fashioned.

"Every Halloween our outhouse would be picked up and carried onto Main Street of downtown Pettisville. All of my friends would joke and laugh as my face burned with embarrassment. I just wanted to hide or disappear. My dad would go downtown and he and some friends would carry it back home."

Donna now laughs at this story, but at the time it was devastating. Poverty impacted her self-esteem and confidence. She knew the shame of her dad being in jail for a lack of child support. It wasn't until the night the ninth child was born (her) that her dad got a steady job at the Archibald Ladder Factory. It was a night of rejoicing.

After Christmas, when she would hear about all the fancy presents her friends had gotten, she felt shame at the simple, practical gifts she received. Her parents were German and spoke with thick German accents.

"I refused to learn German. I was too ashamed. It was the middle of World War II and we were *fighting* the Germans. I didn't want people to know that my parents spoke German at home. Whenever I had to stand up and read in school, I felt humiliated. I didn't know how to pronounce the words and everyone would laugh and make fun of me."

All of this shame impacted Donna's relationship with God. Born into a strict Mennonite family, she wore simple clothes and a head covering. She remembers her sister Betty being excommunicated from the church because she became a cheerleader at school. She remembers the pastor coming to talk to her mom and how she cried over the pain of her daughter being kicked out of the church.

When Donna became an adult, Father God seemed strict and far away. She tried to be a good wife and mom and grew more accomplished as she worked to help her prosperous husband. But the shame seemed to cling to her. She didn't feel quite accepted by the others at church. Somehow she felt less than everyone else.

She loved God, and she wanted to be closer to Him. In the middle of her life, she began to search for Him through prayer. She quit her job and began to take classes at a local Bible college. She cleared her home office of the work papers and began to make it her place to pray. She dedicated the first part of her day to Bible study and prayer. This created conflict with her husband, who wanted her to be available to him and his business in the mornings.

But Donna made a choice. God was more important than anyone or anything in her life. Eventually her marriage was restored and her husband valued who she had become through the power of prayer.

"I remember a worship event where I had a breakthrough. I went with such a heavy burden. In the middle of the meeting, I remember God saying to my spirit, 'Man cannot bind you anymore; you are free.'" This quiet Mennonite woman, who always wanted to hide, made a public spectacle of herself: She began to scream and stomp her feet and shout, "I'm free! I'm free!"

I know this story intimately, because Donna Mae is my beautiful eighty-year-old mother. I remember hearing about her growing up in shame but being set free by the power of God's love, mercy, and acceptance. The proof of the breakthrough has been in the power of a transformed life. If you have the privilege of spending time around my mom, you will sense the presence of the Holy Spirit. There is not another human being who has taught me more about the power of prayer. In the opening story of this book, it was my mom's prayers that saved our lives. God hears the prayers of a mom. I am so thankful for the power of God that freed my mom from shame.

The Ugly Truth about Shame

Shame is a painful emotion that every human being experiences at some point in life. Silent, deadly shame will pollute your faith in God and your ability to pray. Shame torments people from every social class and puts people in bondage in tangible ways:

Shame makes you feel like you can't overcome your past.
Shame puts you in bondage to a negative self-perception.
Shame blocks you from receiving and giving love.

Shame numbs your emotions and makes it difficult to feel joy.

Shame makes you seek to hide and not stand out in a crowd.

Shame handcuffs you to destructive tendencies or addictions.

Shame makes you settle for mediocre rather than press toward God's best.

Shame holds you captive to an abusive control and manipulation.

Shame blocks your relationship with God and makes it difficult to pray.

Racism and Shame

Whole groups of people have been enslaved and put in bondage because of their race. During World War II, Hitler was trying to build a superior race of people defined by the Germanic physical features of blond hair and blue eyes. He believed they held superior intelligence. He perpetrated one of the worst holocausts in history, putting to death the Jews, Christians, and disabled who stood in his way. The "undesirables" were herded into cattle trains and taken to concentration camps, where they were humiliated, robbed, and murdered. Their bodies were abused and used by their captors.

This racist pride of superiority caused everyone who didn't fit the Nazi standard to hide in fear and shame. The evil of racism causes whole groups of people to feel shame for just being who they were made to be.

But Hitler wasn't the first to instill this deep sense of shame on a people. The Enemy has used shame for his purposes since the beginning of time. Another example is the slavery that once ravaged the United States. It began with the greed of those who wanted to use people as property to increase their own wealth. Crowded together in slave ships, many died before arriving in North America from Africa. Those who survived were herded out and sold. They were branded, owned, abused, and shamed.

I'm barely scratching the surface of the systemic evil of racism. Shaming a culture is hell's making.

Every Nation, Every Tribe Free from Shame

God talks about heaven in a way that embraces every tribe and tongue (all cultures). The inhabitants of heaven sing this new song:

> You are worthy to take the scroll and to open its seals, because you were slain, and with your blood you purchased for God persons from every tribe and language and people and nation. You have made them to be a kingdom and priests to serve our God, and they will reign on the earth.
>
> Revelation 5:9–10 NIV

Part of bringing God's kingdom to earth is tearing down cultural racism and bestowing honor and high esteem on every nation, tribe, and tongue. The destructive shame of racism makes people suffer abuse based on their cultural identity. Yet God himself is the one who created every nation and tribe in His image. He is the one creating a kingdom of priests from every culture to serve Him and to reign on the earth.

To rule and reign with God is to have dominion over every issue of life. To reign implies that you and I are considered by God to be part of the majestic rulers of the earth. To have dominion is the ability to rule and reign in a region. God has called us to have dominion on the earth:

> Then God said, "Let us make human beings in our image, to be like us. They will reign over the fish in the sea, the birds in the sky, the livestock, all the wild animals on the earth, and the small animals that scurry along the ground." So God created human beings in his own image.
>
> In the image of God, he created them; male and female he created them. Then God blessed them and said, "Be fruitful and multiply. Fill the earth and govern it. Reign over the fish in the sea, the birds in the sky, and all the animals that scurry along the ground."
>
> Genesis 1:26–28

Queen Esther: A Victim of Circumstance or a Victor of Opportunity?

Queen Esther from the Bible knew the pain of being despised because of her race. Her parents died when she was young. She was a Jewish orphan living in Babylon. She was a prisoner in a foreign land. She knew firsthand the trauma of being brutalized because of her race.

Esther had an opportunity to walk in purity in an impure land. Her rise to power was because of the impetuous banishing of the previous queen, Vashti. The Persian King Ahasuerus, sometimes known by his Greek name *Xerxes*, was the most powerful man in the world. He was holding a banquet for his nobles at the same time that Vashti was holding a banquet for the women. As the men became more intoxicated, the king wanted Vashti to parade in front of this drunken boys' club. Culturally this was an insult. Only concubines remained in the room at the point when the men were drunk.

When Vashti refused, she was banished in a drunken fit of rage. The king had been humiliated in front of all the men. Hastily, she was deposed. Of course, Ahasuerus would regret his decision. When he wanted to find another queen, his advisors devised a plan to choose the most beautiful girl in the kingdom.

Here is where it becomes interesting for *Esther*, which means "star" in Persian. No one except her uncle Mordecai knew that Esther was Jewish. They had hidden this fact to protect her. When Esther was kidnapped and added to the king's harem to be made ready for this beauty contest, Esther likely once again felt violated.

She was in a foreign land without resources to help her. But Esther was not alone. Her uncle Mordecai coached her and she relied on the living God. Esther had a choice in how she would conduct herself in the harem of the king. She not only embraced the beauty treatments, she relied on those in charge to help guide her. When at last she spent time with the king, God's favor was on her and she was chosen to be the bride of the king.

After a number of years, Haman, one of the king's noblemen, sought to annihilate the Jews. He did not know that Queen Esther was Jewish; he simply wanted to get rid of all Jews. At first, Esther may have been tempted to be quiet. But then, convinced by her uncle Mordecai, Esther set out to save her people. Mordecai used these words to compel her to help:

> Do not think in your heart that you will escape in the king's palace any more than all the other Jews. For if you remain completely silent at this time, relief and deliverance will arise for the Jews from another place, but you and your father's house will perish. Yet who knows whether *you have come to the kingdom for such a time as this?*
>
> Esther 4:12–14

Esther implored the Jewish people to fast on her behalf for three days. She instructed them to not even drink water but to cry out to God to save His people. The people responded to her call. They knew it meant life or death. God granted wisdom as to how to approach the king so that Esther not only received his favor, but she received justice. Everything turned around for the people of God because Queen Esther fought on their behalf. Their enemy, Haman, was impaled on the very pole that he had built for Mordecai. The Jewish people overcame their humiliation and shame because of Esther.

God Replaces Shame with Honor

God is the One who replaces your shame with His honor. Along with shame is another partner that the Enemy has to further condemn you, and that is guilt. There is nothing you have ever done that God is not able to cleanse and set you free from.

All of us have fallen short of God's best for our lives. Guilt arises when you commit sin. Your offense violates not only a social code but God's moral code of righteousness. To feel guilty is to experience the negative emotion when you have crossed a moral line and sinned against God and others.

We have all made mistakes. Some sin tries to attach itself to your life and brand your identity. It is a constant struggle in your soul.

Shame will arise after pain and abuse. Your heart has been wounded and so you continue in the pattern of abuse in your own life. You have uncomfortable, awkward feelings and may sometimes have trouble knowing right from wrong. The more you move under the power of sin, the more you will be blinded to the devastation of it. Shame can trap victims in the pain of abuse, twisting their identities.

Brigitte's Story

When I first met Brigitte, I was amazed at the stellar quality of integrity, wisdom, and leadership that she walked in. As a professional woman she has a great deal of favor at her job. She is happily married to her cowboy husband, Gary, and they live on a ranch together. They are a joy to everyone they meet, always praying for others and serving in leadership in the church. I knew prayer was the cornerstone of Brigitte's daily walk with God.

You would never guess that Brigitte was molested year after year by her uncle from the age of nine to seventeen. She felt so much shame, and her uncle warned her that he would go to jail if she said anything. She was in a continual cycle of fear and control. By the time she was sixteen she was pregnant and aborted her first baby. When she was seventeen, she was pregnant again and aborted her second child as well.

"It was only because of God's grace that I ever endured the molestation. There was total brokenness inside me. That's why I made the mistakes that I did with the men that I chose. In fact, I was so broken that I married the same man twice and divorced him twice.

"I really reached the lowest point in my life during my third marriage (second husband). I was never diagnosed with a nervous breakdown, but I truthfully think I was there. My husband was so controlling and manipulating that he wouldn't give me gas for my car or let me have money to buy food to eat.

"When I was in the grocery store, I couldn't even make a decision. The subtle but consistent emotional abuse caused me to second-guess everything. There was so much stress that I would curl up in the corner of the room with a blanket around me just to find peace. I remember my son coming to me to help him edit his paper for school, but my mind was so frazzled that in a whisper I told him that I couldn't do it," Brigitte recalled.

"During this whole situation we were going to church and we put on happy, smiling faces like nothing was going on. Then I went home to the pain. But I would hear the words from my pastor echoing in my mind: 'My grace is sufficient for you.'

"My husband was a firefighter, and everyone knew him and loved him and would never believe that he treated me like he did. When the abuse turned physical and he punched me in the throat full force, I couldn't speak for three days. I knew then I couldn't continue in this marriage.

"Thank God, my children were with their biological dad at the time, so I didn't have to worry about them. I finally just left on foot. I was walking away without anything. I just knew that I had to leave. I called my dad and he could hear it in my voice. I could not continue living under that abusive control.

"The turning point was deciding that I wasn't going to be captive any more. Part of the equation was realizing that I am worth more to my Father in heaven. I didn't need to stay in this hell-on-earth situation.

"God began using His Word to heal me. I attended a Bible college and began meditating on what God's Word says about me. I began to pray God's Word, and I was changing daily to become more like Him.

"I realized that all of my previous choices were the result of my shame. I had thought it was my fault that I was treated this way. My perspective was twisted. I felt like I didn't deserve God's best because something was wrong with me."

The Power of Prayer Demolishes the Lies of Shame

The power of prayer and the study of God's Word pushed out the shame-filled thoughts and feelings that had bound Brigitte since she was a little girl. Now as a woman set free from shame, she boldly helps others walk in freedom.

When you truly know from the depth of your soul that you have been completely forgiven and freed from guilt, sin, and shame, you will find yourself desiring freedom for others. The power of prayer brings deliverance to areas in our lives that are just too twisted for us to untwist or make sense of.

English clergyman, poet, and former slave trader John Newton composed the words to "Amazing Grace" that have captured the hearts of so many:

> Amazing grace, how sweet the sound,
> That saved a wretch like me.
> I once was lost but now am found,
> Was blind, but now I see.[1]

Although Newton had grown up in the church, he became a part of a controlling system that dehumanized people for the gain of money. Newton cried out for mercy when he thought he was going to die during a storm. After this conversion experience, he later left the slave trade and wrote the words to this song to describe God's amazing grace.[2]

God forgives, heals, and restores both those who have been abused and shamed and those who have shamed others. Unless cleansed, healed, and restored, many who have been shamed will find themselves perpetuating the same sin cycle. God's grace is so amazing that it restores and redeems all who cry out for His mercy.

~PRAY~

Amazing God, how wonderful your grace. You made a way of freedom for all who will call on your name. Liberating Friend, I am not alone; you are always at my side. You fought for me when others turned away. You freed me when I could not free myself. Cleansing Spirit, let your fire burn away the dirty rags of my former life.

Begin afresh a humble path of purity and hope. You delivered me from all my pain and shame. Lifter of my Head, help me to live my life filled with your presence, knowing my identity is based on who you are. I'm free to be who you made me to be. Forever, I love you. In your name, Amen.

8

Learning to Pray
with Grace

Knowing who you are in Christ sets you free to be all you were meant to be. God has a purpose for your life. Grace is unmerited favor from God. Grace is God's empowering, redemptive love expressed in action. The first step in learning to pray with grace is to learn who you are in Christ.

1. Read Ephesians 1:1–3. What is the benefit of being united with Christ?
2. Read Ephesians 1:4. Before the foundation of the world, what did God do for you?
3. Write Ephesians 1:5 with your name inserted.
4. Read Ephesians 1:6–12. How is God speaking to you in these verses?

During the expansion of the Roman Empire, when roads were being built, a postal service was developed. Packages would sometimes disappear or arrive damaged. The signet seal was used to safeguard the contents. The package would be examined to make sure that all of the contents were complete. Then hot wax would be poured onto the flap of the envelope or the string of the box and a signet ring of the sender would be pressed into the wax to make a seal. The greater the authority of the signet ring owner, the more apt they were to deliver the package intact.[1]

5. Read Ephesians 1:13. What does it mean to be sealed with the Holy Spirit?

6. Read Ephesians 1:14. Who is the guarantee of your inheritance? What does this mean?

7. Take a posture of prayer such as kneeling or standing. Pray aloud Ephesians 1:15–21. What does it mean for the eyes of your understanding to be enlightened?

8. Read Ephesians 2:1–10 with a pen in hand. Go through this passage and underline every past-tense verb. As you look at the underlined words, what do you hear the Holy Spirit saying to you?

Praying with Confidence, Boldness, and Grace

Confidence, boldness, and grace flow from a crystal-clear calling. Unclear vision and a lack of passion can cause you to hesitate and hold back. Knowing clearly who God is and who you are in Christ will clarify your vision. One of the results of this clarity will be a confidence, boldness, and grace in your prayer life.

9. Read Ephesians 2:8–9 in several different versions of the Bible. What is God revealing to you about His grace?

10. Read Ephesians 3:7. What privilege is given to you by God's grace?

11. Read Romans 3:20–21. What has God done for us?

12. Read Romans 5:17. How does God's promise in this Scripture impact your prayer life?

13. Read, write down, and meditate on Romans 5:20–21. As you contemplate God's promise of grace, spend some time

listening for God's voice. Take the time to write down what you hear Him saying to you. There are downloadable journal pages at www.SueDetweiler.com.

Replacing Shame with Grace

Shame is a dark cloud that comes from the Enemy.

Shame accuses the essence of who you are.

Shame makes you feel like something is wrong with you.

Grace is the rainbow of God's covenant.

Grace brings out the joy of who you are.

Grace is God's gift. You can't earn it, but you can receive it by faith.

The Lies of Shame

Something is wrong with me.

It's all my fault. I'm not good enough.

I will never measure up.

The Truth of God's Grace

Grace is unmerited, undeserved favor.

You have a gift available to you.

Grace frees you from sin.

Grace empowers you to be truly you.

Learning to Pray with Grace

The vicious cycle of shame and guilt cannot totally be relieved by human methods. It takes a supernatural intervention to save us from the depth of this pain. Shame and guilt were paid for on the cross when Jesus died for our sins. Not only was Jesus raised from the dead, but through His grace and forgiveness we are raised with Him to rule and reign.

An orphan mentality develops as we suffer in this world and falsely think we need to do things by our own strength. Learning the joy of dependence as a child of God will transform every orphan heart to find joy in the Father's love. Our Father's love and acceptance free us to depend on Him for help in our time of need.

God is also our bridegroom who lifts the veil of shame from our lives and calls us beautiful and chosen. His tender love cleanses us through His Word. Put your name in this passage of Scripture:

Regarding _____, I can't keep my mouth shut, regarding _____, I can't hold my tongue.

Until her righteousness blazes down like the sun and her salvation flames up like a torch. Foreign countries will see your righteousness, and world leaders your glory.

You'll get a brand-new name straight from the mouth of God.

You'll be a stunning crown in the palm of God's hand, a jeweled gold cup held high in the hand of your God. No more will anyone call you Rejected, and your country will no more be called Ruined. You'll be called Hephzibah (My Delight), and your land Beulah (Married). Because God delights in you and your land will be like a wedding celebration.

For as a young man marries his virgin bride, so your builder marries you,

And as a bridegroom is happy in his bride, so your God is happy with you.

Isaiah 62:1–5 MSG

God is happy with you! You are a delight to Him. He's not ashamed of you. You bring light to His eyes as He cherishes you. You are stunning beside Him. Like a bridegroom with His bride, God can't get enough of you. He looks into your eyes with a smile on His face.

14. As you place your own name in Isaiah 62:1–5, what revelation of God's love and grace do you experience? Take some time and sit in a quiet place with a journal in hand and listen to God's voice as He shares words of love with you. Allow the Holy Spirit to wash over you and heal any pain or shame you may feel. Listen for the sweet sound of the bridegroom wooing you.

Extending God's Grace

Grow in your prayer life by asking God who you can tell what He has shown you in your prayer journal time. Is there someone you know who needs your grace, who needs the grace of God in their life?

For Group Discussion

Bonus Video: Shame comes in all shades. Some we bring on ourselves, but oftentimes it's brought on us through the actions of others. Watch the bonus video at www.SueDetweiler.com.

15. Describe an area of shame you have experienced in your life. How did God empower you with His grace? Are there certain situations that trigger feelings of shame in you presently? In what ways can we pray for you right now?

9

I Am Secure

Transforming Anxiety into Peace

One morning when I was standing at the kitchen sink, my hands in dishwater, my husband, Wayne, said, "Sue, we got the announcement yesterday. American Eagle Airlines is closing its doors in Nashville. Everyone is being laid off."

Panic began to spread up the back of my neck. This had been a second job for Wayne to supplement our income as pastors. However, we had resigned the church that we pastored for nine years and were in transition. This was the job that was helping to feed our four daughters, ages six, four, two, and newborn.

I was silent for a moment as my mind raced. *What are we going to do? How are we going to live? I need to stay home with our daughters. I can't get a job now.*

I shook the dishwater off my hands and turned to Wayne, praying for words that would help. I sensed God giving me the words to encourage my faithful husband:

"Honey, it must mean that promotion is around the corner for you." There was a precious moment of peace reflected in my hardworking husband's eyes. He was thankful for my words. He knew I believed in him. He was working overtime to make ends meet.

Reeling from the news, I took off for my early-morning prayer walk. I gave God my long list of concerns. As I prayed I started to become more anxious as the reality of our situation began to set in. I ended my conversation with "And God, we need groceries!"

As I moved through my morning routine with my daughters, I was surprised at lunchtime when an acquaintance showed up with four bags of groceries. She didn't know that my husband was losing his job, but God did. My new friend simply said, "I was praying this morning, and God just put you guys on my heart. I thought you might need this." Tears filled my eyes as I received her inspired act of kindness.

I was amazed at God's specific answer to my prayer, and peace began to fill my anxious heart. *God, if you can answer my simple, faith-filled request for groceries, you can do anything!*

As I put the groceries away in our pantry, God reminded me of my prayer the week before. I had visited Wayne at the airport where he worked. The job had been great as a secondary income for our growing family. We especially appreciated the flying benefits that enabled us to visit our extended families.

I had been watching Wayne work in the cold, dark room where he threw bags on a conveyer belt, and I cried out to God in prayer: *My husband is made for more than this. He is a seminary graduate. You have made him to pastor people. Lord, get my husband out of here!*

Now here we were a week later. Oops. I didn't mean for Wayne to lose his job. I was asking God to promote him. That's why the words *"promotion must be around the corner"* came out of my mouth. I was able to say those words because I had been praying them over my husband.[1]

How do you keep your anxious thoughts from becoming a toxic swamp in your mind, polluting everyone around you? I have a one-word answer: *prayer.*

Doing Life with Jesus

Two of the best-known sisters in the Bible, Mary and Martha, approached life with Jesus in different ways, as illustrated in Luke:

> As Jesus and the disciples continued on their way to Jerusalem, they came to a certain village where a woman named Martha welcomed him into her home. Her sister, Mary, sat at the Lord's feet, listening to what he taught. But Martha was distracted by the big dinner she was preparing. She came to Jesus and said, "Lord, doesn't it seem unfair to you that my sister just sits here while I do all the work? Tell her to come and help me."
>
> But the Lord said to her, "My dear Martha, you are worried and upset over all these details! There is only one thing worth being concerned about. Mary has discovered it, and it will not be taken away from her."
>
> 10:38–42

Martha was the oldest and the owner of the home that Jesus came to. We don't know if Martha inherited the home; we just know she was the responsible one. She was the hostess distracted by the big dinner she was preparing. Martha was concerned about *serving Jesus.*

Mary drew close to Jesus, sitting at His feet. She was unconcerned about food. She wanted to spend every moment with Him. Her desire was intimacy. She wanted to listen to each word He spoke and linger in the joy of the moment. Mary was concerned about *being with Jesus.* She wanted to learn from Him.

Jesus cut through the cultural and religious expectations of the day and called women close to Him in intimate conversation. He showed that he valued Mary's ability to think, reason, and carry on intellectual dialogue. His very conversation challenged the rabbinical thinking of the day: A woman was the property of a man and not worth the time to teach. Women were viewed as inferior, but Jesus valued and esteemed both Mary and Martha.

Martha's activity appears anxious. Preparing a meal in that day took a lot of effort. She also seems concerned about propriety.

The prescribed role of women was to be in the kitchen. It may have irritated Martha not only that Mary was not helping her in the kitchen, but that she had overstepped her role as a woman.

Jesus was not concerned with pretense; He wanted personal relationship. I love His words to Martha:

> My dear Martha, you are worried and upset over all these details! There is only one thing worth being concerned about. Mary has discovered it, and it will not be taken away from her.
>
> Luke 10:41–42

It seems like Jesus is making a play on words. He may mean, *Martha, why are you doing unnecessary work preparing a feast of many dishes, when **one dish is enough?** Or He may be saying, **The one thing** that is most important is spending time at my feet like Mary.* Jesus' words are surprising.

The key to prayer is learning to have intimate conversations with Jesus. Jesus affirmed this when He said, "Mary has discovered it, and it will not be taken away from her" (Luke 10:42). Mary chose the better part, and so can you and I.

Even though Mary went against societal expectations, she chose the most precious part of life, an intimate relationship with God. Even though she neglected her duties, she found what was most important. She refused to be robbed of the *joy* of being with Jesus.

Our perspective would dramatically shift if we stopped thinking about the *duty* of having a quiet time. When we have a mental religious list (or sometimes it is written in ink) of the things we need to get done, we take on prayer like one more thing we have to do to please God.

Truth be told, most women have both Mary and Martha lurking within their hearts. Whenever I listen to someone who brags about spending hours and hours of time with Jesus I find myself a bit suspicious. In my skeptical mind I find myself wondering, *Is there someone else stressed out, carrying it all—helping this one whose head is in the clouds?* I know that my husband and daughters have sometimes felt that way with me. They carry so many practical things in our household. If I'm Mary, I need a bunch of Marthas walking beside me.

In Jesus' last words to His disciples, He warned them that life would not always be smooth sailing. But He also promised them peace.

> I have told you these things, so that in Me you may have [perfect] peace. In the world you have tribulation and distress and suffering; but be courageous [be confident, be undaunted, be filled with joy]; I have overcome the world. [My conquest is accomplished, My victory abiding.]
>
> John 16:33 AMP

Jesus gave us His Word so that you and I can have perfect peace and confidence. In the same breath, He promised that we would have tribulation, trials, distress, and frustration. Then He instructs us to take courage, be confident, certain, undaunted!

How can He expect you to be undaunted in the midst of distress? He simply says, "I have overcome the world!" He is the overcomer. He will help you overcome every trial. At the cross, He deprived the Enemy of power over you. Whatever situation you are presently facing, it has no power to harm you. He conquered it for you. This just makes me want to shout! His promise of peace in our lives is not a rinky-dink promise of superficial pats on the back. He walks with us through trying situations. He is the Prince of Peace, so if you walk with Him, you will experience His peace.

To be secure means that you are free from danger or harm. You are safe. To be secure in this storm-filled world means that you have replaced your worry and anxiety with God's peace. You have found a protected harbor in your mind, will, and emotions. Your life is lived firmly established with a certainty of God's goodness.

The Promise of Peace

If there were a pass code to avoid every toxic relationship and traumatic event you are going to experience in your life, then you would not grow to be the person of depth and maturity that God has destined you to be. God is not the author of pain and suffering; He is the deliverer. It is the Word of God that is sharper than any sword and can divide between the soul and spirit (Hebrews 4:12). Rather than taking you around the pain, He will show you the way through it.

I am not writing this book to sound like I am now free from all trials, and I have arrived at the safe harbor of peace! In this world, we all face trials. The good news is we don't go through it alone. Jesus is the One who is in the boat with us. He is the One calming the storm. So cry out to Him in prayer.

To replace your anxiety with His unshakable peace requires that you trust Him. Choose to take heart and put your focus on the fact that Jesus overcame, so you can too. He is the God of peace who crushes anxiety under your feet: "The God of peace will soon crush Satan under your feet. May the grace of our Lord Jesus be with you" (Romans 16:20).

God gives His grace to you in times of your greatest need. His unmerited favor surprises me every time. It never fails to amaze me how God chooses to answer my prayers.

Don't Give Up!

Anxiety is a deceiver. Like a blowfish that expands to make itself look bigger than it really is, anxiety exaggerates every bad thing that could happen. Worry will convince you that you can't make it.

One day when my children were still young, I pushed my stroller in my neighborhood and I met another mom. I visited with her and her children in their home for about an hour. Since my husband and I were pastors, our neighborhood felt like a "parish" to me, so I regularly made "house calls" on neighbors. Our neighborhood was a suburb of new homes with white picket fences and hopes for the future.

My neighbor appeared stressed, but nothing out of the ordinary compared to the other moms I visited. Her daughters were beautiful, with golden hair. They loved play jewelry, ribbons, and Barbies. After that initial meeting, I kept in touch with the mom, but only by waving my hand or sharing brief words on the street as I walked by, pushing my baby stroller.

Then one morning, I awoke to the tragic news that she had taken her life and the lives of her children. She had driven her car, with her children, into a nearby lake, and everyone drowned. I share her story here, not remembering her name or even the exact number of children involved or the details of their deaths twenty years ago. I feel regret that I did not do more to help her.[2]

Whatever you are facing in life, it is important not to give up! Sometimes we need to put one foot in front of the other and trust God that He will help us through the difficult times. "Let us not become weary in doing good, for at the proper time we will reap a harvest if we do not give up" (Galatians 6:9 NIV).

Peace through the Seasons of Life

The Enemy may provide a counterfeit way to avoid pain. Often he uses addiction to make you feel a temporary relief from internal torment. The alcohol, drugs, sugar, or sexual release provides a moment of forgetting the pain and experiencing pleasure. The hook of the addiction is that it takes more and more of your drug of choice to experience the high.

Sometimes the pain is simply boredom or a discontent in your season of life. Right this moment I am writing by a pool and four little girls are playing with their dad and mom. A moment of missing my girls, who are now adults, stabs my heart. Yet when I was in the season of raising my children, who came at two-year intervals, I was too tired to really enjoy them. Why do we long for a different season rather than embracing the sweetness of the season we are in?

God's peace and perspective bring us through the mundane, the terrible, and the terrific with His grace and wisdom. The key to enjoying your daily life is to seek God in prayer, letting Him set your priorities. Listening to His voice will always lead you to value what is truly important.

I remember fasting and praying about how to educate our children. We heard Him clearly. I was to lay down my own desires and freedoms to spend my time homeschooling our children. At that point of surrendering my own will to God's will, I had no idea that I would have fifteen years of experience leading a homeschool academy that my children all attended. I homeschooled for eighteen years and got to see not only my children but the other children at the academy grow in grace and wisdom. Now my daughter Angela Grace teaches Spanish at the same academy where she learned to love languages.

Prayer instructs us on which way we should go. Prayer helps us make good choices at the crossroads of our journey. When you don't know which way to go, stop and listen to God's voice instruct you on the path you should take.

Finding Peace in Your Daily Life

In this Instagram-perfect world, it may appear that your neighbor has a beautiful life while yours is filled with stress. It's important that you don't compare her outward appearance with your internal struggle. You really don't know what she is going through.

It's difficult to describe the anxiety and pressures of our last few years. Life is a walk of faith, and it takes twists and turns that you are not expecting. After twenty-eight years of pastoring in Nashville, we knew that God was calling us to a new territory, but we didn't know exactly where. We stepped out in faith and explored an opportunity in Virginia and then in North Carolina. Then I was awakened with a vision of the state of Texas surrounded in flames and a compelling call from God to plant a new church in Texas.

That may sound exciting and glamorous, but we didn't know anyone in Texas. Though our denomination opened doors and encouraged us to plant, we were starting all over. That meant pulling up roots and moving into the unknown. The hardest part for me was leaving my adult daughters.

My mom helped me when I was anxious and torn up about being away from my daughters and sons-in-law. She was out walking with me, and I shared with her what we were praying about. She stopped walking and looked at me and said, "Sue, you have raised your daughters. You don't know where they will end up. God has a call on your life. You need to obey God and walk through these open doors."

It's just like a praying mom to speak peace to an anxious heart.

We saw God do miracle after miracle as He provided for us and confirmed His call. Make no mistake. Church planting from scratch is not easy. In fact, it is lonely. Thank goodness our adult children helped us drive our stuff across the country and move in, but then we had to say good-bye to them as they headed back to Tennessee. I cried. I was away from my daughters for their birthdays and for special events. Yes, I am a frequent flyer to Tennessee, but it is still tough.

We opened our hands and let our adult children fly, trusting God that He would provide for them, care for them, lead them, and guide them. Now our youngest daughter, Sarah Faith, has moved to Texas and is going to college, working, and living at home. Our oldest daughter, Rachel Joy, her husband, Dustin, and our handsome grandson, Andrew Wayne, will be moving to Texas in a few months. We are thrilled that God has called them here.

God is so good. As a mom, I have wasted far too much time and emotional energy worrying about things that I can't control anyway. Fretting is a waste of energy. If your prayer time leaves you feeling more stressed than peaceful, then you are not casting your cares on Him in prayer.

When I was growing up, Scripture songs were very popular. Putting Scripture to music helps me memorize and recall the Word of God from long ago. My aunt Joyce and her daughters would sing and harmonize these words:

> God is our refuge and strength, a very present help in trouble. Therefore, will not we fear, though the earth be removed, and though the mountains be carried into the midst of the sea.
>
> Psalm 46:1–2 KJV

At the time, Joyce had gone through a divorce that she didn't want and was a single mother raising four children. She was making the decision of whether to marry again or remain a single mother. She gained strength and wisdom by singing her prayers to God. Now she is a grandma of many and has seen God provide for all of her needs as a single mom.

What's the song in your heart? What Scripture are you standing on in your time of need? You will know the Scripture because it will jump off the page into your life. Immediate peace, hope, and perspective will guide you in your decision making.

Before you reach the harbor of peace in your mind, you will often have to follow the wisdom of these words: "Give all your worries and cares to God, for he cares about you" (1 Peter 5:7).

Giving God *all your worries and cares* will often mean you have to cast them away from you. You have to make a deliberate choice not to wallow in the torment of indecision, regret, or fear.

Walk in God's Peace

To walk in God's peace, I need to regularly detoxify my mind and emotions. Here is a list of detoxifying habits that have helped restore God's peace in my life:

Reading the Bible (Replacing the world's words with God's Word)
Prayer and Meditation (Replacing my concerns with God's care)

Forgiveness (Replacing my hurt with God's health)
Journaling (Reframing tough situations with God's strategy)
Church Community (Replacing my apathy with God's passion)
Books (Replacing my confusion with God's clarity)
Podcasts (Restoring my foggy brain with God's focus)
Conferences (Reshaping my weakness with God's power)
Counseling (Rebuilding my brokenness with God's wholeness)[3]

God's peace establishes order and balance in your life and home. God's peace is a tangible force that overwhelms overwrought emotions with God's powerful presence. His peace anchors your thoughts and steadies your emotions. His peace strengthens your ability to face stress-filled situations with calm serenity. Replacing your anxiety with God's peace is a moment-by-moment choice to view God as bigger than your problem. God's peace is the absence of inner conflict and turmoil. God's peace is embracing the character of Jesus, who is the Prince of Peace.

~PRAY~

Prince of Peace, Shepherd of my heart and soul, lead me in your ways.

Guide me on your paths. Help me to turn away from the swamp of anxiety, worry, and dread. Show me how to live peace-filled, tranquil days. Thank you for healthy thoughts and reflections. I will meditate on what is noble and right. I know that as I pray about everything, your peace will guard my heart and mind. Your peace exceeds anything I could understand. So I will fix my mind on what is lovely. I will celebrate what is admirable. Daily, I rejoice in your peace (Philippians 4:4–8). Amen.

10

Learning to Pray with Peace

I am so excited to walk with you through these Scriptures. If you consistently struggle with worry and anxiety, I want to pray for you:

Precious Lord, I pray for my friend as she reads this book and walks in faith. Father, anoint her right now with peace. In the name of Jesus, we take authority over every demonic stronghold that has distracted, discouraged, and depressed. I pray for an electric bolt of hope to energize her mind and heart as she reads these Scriptures and answers these questions. Let this be a time of real breakthrough in her prayer life. Holy Spirit, help this lesson to be a springboard of greater revelation led and guided by you. In Jesus' name we pray, amen.

1. Read Isaiah 26:3. What is the key to being kept in perfect peace according to this Scripture?
2. Read Isaiah 26:4. What do you learn about God's character in this verse?

3. Read Psalm 37. Mark the words that repeat in this chapter. What do these words tell you about the focus of the psalm?

4. Psalm 37 is written by David as an acrostic with each segment beginning with a different letter of the Hebrew alphabet. This method was likely used as a tool of memorization, communicating the need to remember the words of Psalm 37 and apply them to your daily life. In your own words, what do you think is important to apply to your life in these verses?

5. Go back and read more slowly Psalm 37:1–2. According to this passage, why are we tempted to fret? What happens to those who do evil?

6. Read Psalm 37:3–4. The word for heart in Hebrew is *leb*, which means "heart, intellect, awareness, mind, inner person, inner feelings, deepest thoughts, inner self."[1] As you reflect deeply on verses 3 and 4, what is God calling you to do? What are you promised?

7. Read Psalm 37:5. Notice the word that is often translated commit. In the Hebrew this word is *galal*, which means to "roll away" or "remove." "The picture is of a camel, burdened with a heavy load; when the load is to be removed, the camel kneels down, tilts far to one side, and the load rolls off."[2] With this understanding, read Psalm 37:5 again. How does this apply to your prayer life?

8. When we are not able to control a situation, we can become anxious. Read Psalm 37:6. What does this Scripture promise you?

9. Read Psalm 37:7. How does God call you to pray when life is not fair?

10. Read Psalm 37:8. Now, look back: How many times has this chapter instructed you to not fret or worry? To fret in the Hebrew is *charah* and means "to heat" or "inflame oneself." The word *charah* is often applied to worry and frustration that leads to anger.[3] In addition to not worrying, what does Psalm 37:8 call you to do?

11. Read Psalm 37:9. What will happen to those who are evil? What promise do you have if you hope in the Lord?

12. Read Psalm 37:10–11. What promises are repeated in these verses? (Both a positive and a negative promise.)

13. Read Psalm 37:12–13. How do these verses bring perspective to your issues?

14. Read Psalm 37:14–15. How will God protect you?

15. Read Psalm 37:16–17. Have you worried about not having enough? What are you promised?

16. Read Psalm 37:18–22. How do these verses underscore and repeat what has already been promised?

17. Read Psalm 37:23–26. What does God promise about legacy?

18. Read Psalm 37:27–33. What new insights do you gain as His promises are repeated?

19. Read Psalm 37:34–40. What fresh revelation do you have in these verses?

20. Now go back and make a list of the negative promises for the wicked and the positive promises for those who hope in God. Make a list of the actions that you are supposed to take to walk in hope.

Gaining God's Perspective

I hope this exercise of looking at Psalm 37 has enlightened your heart with revelation and perspective. You are not alone. God is going to bring vindication and justice in your life. You don't have to strive or fight for yourself. He is going to fight for you. If you consistently delight in God and find your refuge in Him, you will prosper and the evil will be judged.

21. Read Philippians 4:6. The Greek word for worry is *meri-mao* and means "'to divide into parts.' The words suggest a distraction, a preoccupation with things causing anxiety,

stress, and pressure. Jesus speaks against worry and anxiety because of the watchful care of a heavenly father who is ever mindful of our daily needs."[4] With this in mind, what are you instructed to do in verse 6? If the Scripture tells you to do something, is God's grace there to help you do it?

22. Read Philippians 4:7. What is God's promise to you?

Putting God's Word into Action

I first memorized Philippians 4:6–7 when I was a junior in high school. I was first string on the varsity volleyball team. My starting position was middle back, which meant that I would likely receive the first serve of the game. I would move my feet and get in ready position to receive the ball and remember these verses. I needed God's peace to guard my mind. These words became living and active for me. I will never forget the power of renewing my mind as I meditated on and memorized God's Word.

23. Think about the most difficult situation you are facing right now. It could be a strained relationship, financial stress, or job-related anxiety. It's the type of thing that keeps you up at night being tempted to think negative thoughts. After you have the situation in mind, read Philippians 4:8 out loud. How do these words impact how you process the difficulty you are facing?

24. Read Philippians 4:9. Is there a role model in your life who walks in peace? How would he or she handle the situation you are facing? What does God promise you in Philippians 4:9?

Praying with Confidence, Boldness, and Grace

God has your back. He wouldn't promise His peace to guard your heart and mind if it wasn't possible. His peace truly transcends your understanding. However, His peace is not always your first experience. You may first feel the torment that the Enemy sends your way as you think about the bad things that could happen. If you meditate on what the Enemy is feeding your mind, his lies will steal your peace.

If you are like me, you may also struggle with the temptation to try to escape the pressure and the stress by turning to things that comfort you, like activity, movies, books, and food. Or you may have harmful temptations or addictions like masturbation, pornography, drinking, or drugs. It may be the type of thing that you did for enjoyment before you were saved. When life gets tough, you find yourself going back to those momentary pleasures.

25. What do you turn to for comfort rather than God? Does it work?

26. If you find yourself addicted to something, what is it?

27. Ask the Holy Spirit for a strategy to deal with stress rather than turning to your counterfeit comfort. Write down the strategy as the Holy Spirit reveals it.

Getting free is a process. Staying free is a lifelong journey. *Prayer is the fuel that fires the passion to stay close to God* when you and I get anxious. Recently, when I was in the middle of a stress-filled situation, I heard the Holy Spirit encourage me through this quote: "Cows run away from the storm while the buffalo charges toward it—and gets through it quicker. Whenever I'm confronted with a tough challenge, I do not prolong the torment, I become the buffalo."[5] The Holy Spirit's direction and guidance can show us how to be like the buffalo and turn into the storm.

God's peace is like being in the eye of the storm. In His presence there is fullness of joy. The more responsibility you carry, the more you need to stay close to the presence of God to help you face the storm.

Replacing Anxiety with Peace

Worry frustrates and steals your peace.

Fretting inflames a situation with anger.

Anxiety and stress lead to all types of illness.

The temptation to turn to addictions increases in times of stress.

Peace leads to joy and productivity in your life.

Being still in God's presence and trusting Him transforms your perspective.

Those who make God their refuge will walk in peace.

Lies of Anxiety

Anxiety lies to you and points to quick fixes or counterfeit comforts.

Anxiety can trap you in a self-fulfilling prophecy of failure.

Anxiety gives you a false perspective that seems real.

The Enemy is the author of anxiety.

Truth of Peace

Peace trusts God to fulfill His promise.

Peace anchors its hope in God.

Peace meditates on and magnifies God's Word.

Peace brings God's perspective.

God's presence always brings peace.

Extending God's Grace

Do you have a prayer partner? Ask God to send you someone with whom you can link arms and pray daily.

For Group Discussion

Bonus Video: The day I stopped being a cow and transformed into a buffalo. Watch this chapter's bonus video at www.SueDetweiler.com.

28. Describe an area of worry you are presently facing in your life. Are you in the middle of the anxious torment, or have you discovered God's peace? Are there addictive types of temptations creating a counterfeit comfort in your life? Do you tend to be more like a cow or a buffalo in a storm? In what ways can we pray for you right now?

—11—

I Am Transformed

Transforming Sadness into Joy

"Just because you grow up in a church doesn't make you a Christian," said Marta. As a Bible teacher, missionary, and evangelist, Marta exudes love for Jesus. The knowledge of His Word flows from her heart. We were out to dinner when she shared her story.

"I was twenty-nine years old and at my lowest. I was lying in an abortion clinic after my fourth abortion, looking over my life. Sure, I had been a successful marketer for television with a lot of money and prestige. At one point, I had lived in a 14,000-square-foot home with my boyfriend. He had two lake homes and three boats. We were *living the life*. When I was at this high point, I had no thoughts about the choices I was making.

"But now as I lay in this cold abortion clinic, I began to remember words from Scripture that had made their way into my life. You see, my parents took me to church every time the doors opened. Yet my rebellion was hidden under my beautifully made-up face and carefully manicured nails.

"Underneath the superficial beauty was a wounded seven-year-old who had been abused by my neighbor. My mother had warned me never to go near this person, but I didn't listen. When the abuse happened, I felt like it was all my fault. So I didn't tell anyone. I just suffered in silence.

"The most terrible thing that happened in those days of my life was that I didn't get caught. I could be driving down the road extremely drunk, thinking in my mind that I shouldn't be doing this because someone could get hurt—but I did it anyway.

"It was like my life was flashing before my eyes as I lay in this abortion recovery room. Sorrow and loss flooded over me as I looked back at my life. I remembered the abortion when I was seventeen. I remember leaving home and getting married at eighteen. I was starting to sink. I needed a change in my life."

Sadness Depletes Your Strength[1]

Did you ever wake up and just feel down? Did it take effort to just get out of bed? When you looked at your day, did it feel monotonous and mundane? Everything you ate was tasteless. Everything you attempted seemed pointless. You just wanted to escape into a constant apathetic slumber.

Sadness is emotional pain characterized by the feeling of loss, despair, or helplessness. Sadness is considered to be a short-term lowering of your mood. Depression is when the low mood persists and becomes chronic or unceasing.

In a practical sense, sadness may be a result of any of the following:

Fatigue: You may just be overly tired. Stress can cause emotional fatigue. Stressors can range from the loss of a loved one or concern for your finances, to loss of a job or worry over your child.

Low Serotonin: Serotonin is a hormone in the body that impacts appetite, sleep, memory, temperature, and mood. Women dealing with depression often have low serotonin levels. Periods of stress often make it difficult to eat right or exercise, which will cause low serotonin in your body.

Loss, Sadness, Depression: Along with physical factors, dwelling on negative thoughts and events can extend sadness. Constant feelings of hopelessness, anxiety, and emptiness that persist for weeks and months may be a sign of clinical depression. Seek professional help if depression continues or if suicidal thoughts occur. If these feelings prevent your normal functioning, you may be dealing with clinical depression.

Transformation Often Begins at Our Lowest Point

Transformation doesn't happen until we realize that we need a change in our lives. Sometimes the deepest sorrow is over those things that we are powerless to change, like the death of someone we love. Other times it is realizing that our lives need more purpose and direction.

Change for Marta took place when she was at her lowest. "As I lay on the abortion table, waiting for the father of the child that I had just aborted to pick me up, God began to speak to me. He showed me three men in the Bible: Moses, David, and Paul. All of these men had killed someone, just as I had killed my babies. God spoke to my heart: If He could transform their lives and use them He could change me and use me.

"*Jesus, if you could forgive them, you can forgive me. Use me, I pray.* That simple prayer was the beginning of the turnaround in my life. This horrible day became the best day of my life as I remembered God's Word: 'For God so loved the world that He gave His only begotten Son, that whoever believes in Him should not perish but have everlasting life' (John 3:16 NKJV).

"I made a choice that day to receive God's precious gift as my own. I knew that Jesus had died on the cross for my sins, but this was the first day that I received His redemption as my own."

Encountering Jesus Changes Everything

Listening to Marta's story reminded me that God is able to reach us at our lowest point and change our lives. No one is out of the reach of God's power to change their lives. Encountering God in our daily lives changes our perspective.

I am reminded of the story of the Samaritan woman when she encountered Jesus at the well. Jesus, led by the Spirit, knew that He must go through Samaria. He models for us the call to be available for divine appointments. Normally, you didn't go to the well in the heat of the day. The fact that the woman was there at that time likely indicates that she was avoiding being around the other women. It was customary for women to go early in the day so they could avoid the heat and have time to fellowship. John 4 shares the story of their encounter.

Jesus, worn out by the trip, sat down at the well. It was noon.

A woman, a Samaritan, came to draw water. Jesus said, "Would you give me a drink of water?" (His disciples had gone to the village to buy food for lunch.)

The Samaritan woman, taken aback, asked, "How come you, a Jew, are asking me, a Samaritan woman, for a drink?" (Jews in those days wouldn't be caught dead talking to Samaritans.)

Jesus answered, "If you knew the generosity of God and who I am, you would be asking me for a drink, and I would give you fresh, living water."

The woman said, "Sir, you don't even have a bucket to draw with, and this well is deep. So how are you going to get this 'living water'? Are you a better man than our ancestor Jacob, who dug this well and drank from it, he and his sons and livestock, and passed it down to us?"

Jesus said, "Everyone who drinks this water will get thirsty again and again. Anyone who drinks the water I give will never thirst—not ever. The water I give will be an artesian spring within, gushing fountains of endless life."

The woman said, "Sir, give me this water so I won't ever get thirsty, won't ever have to come back to this well again!"

He said, "Go call your husband and then come back."

"I have no husband," she said.

"That's nicely put: 'I have no husband.' You've had five husbands, and the man you're living with now isn't even your husband. You spoke the truth there, sure enough."

"Oh, so you're a prophet! Well, tell me this: Our ancestors worshiped God at this mountain, but you Jews insist that Jerusalem is the only place for worship, right?"

"Believe me, woman, the time is coming when you Samaritans will worship the Father neither here at this mountain nor there in Jerusalem. You worship guessing in the dark; we Jews worship in the clear light of day. God's way of salvation is made available through the Jews. But the time is coming—it has, in fact, come—when what you're called will not matter and where you go to worship will not matter.

"It's who you are and the way you live that count before God. Your worship must engage your spirit in the pursuit of truth. That's the kind of people the Father is out looking for: those who are simply and honestly themselves before him in their worship. God is sheer being itself—Spirit. Those who worship him must do it out of their very being, their spirits, their true selves, in adoration."

The woman said, "I don't know about that. I do know that the Messiah is coming. When he arrives, we'll get the whole story."

"I am he," said Jesus. "You don't have to wait any longer or look any further."

Just then his disciples came back. They were shocked. They couldn't believe he was talking with that kind of a woman. No one said what they were all thinking, but their faces showed it.

The woman took the hint and left. In her confusion she left her water pot. Back in the village she told the people, "Come see a man who knew all about the things I did, who knows me inside and out. Do you think this could be the Messiah?" And they went out to see for themselves.

vv. 6–30 MSG

Brokenness and Sorrow Are Healed in God's Presence

We don't know all that the Samaritan woman experienced as a girl, but God does. We don't know how old she was or even her

113

name. Yet she had the longest recorded one-on-one conversation with Jesus. Jesus crossed lines of propriety to speak to her. Jews didn't speak with Samaritans. Nor did a man speak with a woman without her husband present. A rabbi certainly wouldn't speak to a woman who had a questionable character.

Jesus drew the woman into a spiritual conversation by pointing to her daily human need to drink water. He enticed her to thirst for spiritual water that would quench her deepest desires. Of course she wanted this *living water.*

Jesus spoke the truth in love, "Go call your husband and then come back." Jesus constantly breaks through our barriers to help us encounter Him. He met her where she was at. She had had five husbands, and now the man she was with wasn't even her husband. Her sin was revealed, so she changed the subject. She picked a topic of theological debate of the day: how and where could they worship God. It was easier for her to talk about religion than about relationship. She was focusing on the law, but Jesus showed her grace.

Because she was a woman, and a person with a poor reputation, the disciples were shocked that Jesus would be with her alone by the well. Likely she had few, if any, women friends. She went to the well alone in the middle of the day rather than suffer rejection by going when the other women went early in the morning. She was an outcast, unworthy to approach God. So God, in human form, approached her.

She was from a despised race. Samaritans were thought of as half-breeds, having a mixture of Jewish ancestry and other nationalities that had repopulated within their borders. They were seen as dogs by devout Jews who looked down on them. Jesus reached beyond the boundaries of race to reach the needs of her heart. He not only prophesied about her present condition, he pointed to a time when salvation would be available to everyone.

Jesus revealed himself to the Samaritan woman, and she received Him as the Messiah, the anointed one sent by God. She didn't go through a lengthy twelve-step process to be delivered. She entered into Jesus' one-step program of being lost, then found by Him.

She became one of the first evangelists, saying, "'Come see a man who knew all about the things I did, who knows me inside and out. Do you think this could be the Messiah?' And they went out to see for themselves" (John 4:30 MSG).

The conviction that comes when we are face-to-face with Jesus draws us closer to Him. When we encounter God intimately, we don't want any barriers between us. There is great power in having the God of the universe know everything about you and still want to be in relationship with you. To be known, accepted, and loved powerfully changes each one of us from the inside out.

The Power of a Changed Life

Marta's life, like the Samaritan woman's, was powerfully changed. She wanted to understand theologically what God was saying. The fact that there were three men in the Bible who had also murdered encouraged her that He could use her even though she had killed four babies through abortion.

"I began to pray desperately to know God. I asked Him to take me to a place where I could learn His Word. I wanted to know what God said about God. I pressed in to know Him as He is. I wanted to know the joy of being in His presence. I was tired of my superficial life. I believe God's Word when it says, 'Jesus is the same yesterday, today, and forever' (Hebrews 13:8).

"As I believed this Scripture, I began to pray for the same miracles that Jesus walked in. The real question in prayer is, Do you believe His Word? I believe that when I pray God's Word, I am praying His will, and I will receive what I ask for.

"In addition to praying God's Word, I take time to listen. If this is a real conversation, then I need to believe God responds to my prayers. He will speak to me and direct me.

"I get my cup of tea and blanket, curl up, and get in the Word of God. I always pray for wisdom and ask the Lord to speak to me before I read His Word. A relationship is a back-and-forth conversation.

"You can't build a friendship with God with a one-way conversation. We need to hear His voice to direct us in the days ahead. We need to recognize Him in the Word and to have His perspective—to see with His eyes and hear with His ears."

Transformation Impacts the Way You Think

The process of transformation can be a long journey, where the Word of God is your guidebook and prayer is your footpath. In the midst of your walk with God, at some point you will have to confront the way you think.

When you are in the middle of a painful situation, you must believe that life will get better. We get stuck when we don't know what's coming next. Facts shout convincingly as negative thoughts bombard us: *Things will never change. I will always struggle with this. I will never get better.*

One afternoon I was struggling with these negative thoughts, and I decided to talk to my mom, who is a spunky lady. As I admitted my negative thoughts to my mom, she put her hand on her hip, shook her head to one side and said, "Sue, you are in *stinkin' thinkin'*." The way she said it made me laugh, but the truth of her words stuck with me.

Stinkin' thinkin' is a downward staircase leading to a dark place in our emotions. When you are stuck in this dungeon of dreary thoughts, it will impact every area of your life. You can't afford to get stuck in a funk for long. The people you love will know something is wrong by the way you are irritable and hard to please. I define a FUNK like this:

F—Floundering
U—Under
N—Negative
K—Knowledge

In a FUNK your mind is spiraling out of control. One negative thought leads to the next. You may have some "knowledge" about a negative fact. But as you exaggerate the facts in your mind, they do not add up to the truth.

Get Out of Your FUNK

The key to getting out of your FUNK is to reshape your thinking. God's Word is the most powerful tool you can use to change your thoughts to His thoughts. Second Corinthians gives us great insight on our thoughts:

> We are human, but we don't wage war as humans do. We use God's mighty weapons, not worldly weapons, to knock down the strongholds of human reasoning and to destroy false arguments. We destroy every proud obstacle that keeps people from knowing God. We capture their rebellious thoughts and teach them to obey Christ.
>
> 2 Corinthians 10:3–5

If you are in a FUNK, you believe a lie that makes you afraid. At the core of your problem are thoughts that you need to capture. Make your thoughts obey God's thoughts.

Every day we have the opportunity to agree with God and allow His perspective to flood us with His hope. It's like having a pressure washer in your mind. You have a choice to reshape your negative thoughts and replace them with a positive mindset. This does not mean that you and I will not experience emotional pain and loss. In fact, it is the pain that we experience in life that shapes our character to be more like Christ, who was crucified for our sake. Jesus suffered the shame of the cross, yet knew that joy was His inheritance. Joy and honor await every obedient heart that runs the race of faith and doesn't give up.

You Are Not Alone

The good news is that you are not alone. If you are presently in the pits, there is One who can reach down into the lowest place and bring you comfort. Like a gentle shepherd He will walk in the valley with you as you pour out your emotions in prayer:

> The Lord is my shepherd; I shall not want. He makes me to lie down in green pastures; He leads me beside the still waters. He restores my soul; He leads me in the paths of righteousness for His name's sake. Yea, though I walk through the valley of the shadow of death, I will fear no evil; for You are with me; Your rod and Your staff, they comfort me. You prepare a table before me in the presence of my enemies; You anoint my head with oil; my cup runs over. Surely goodness and mercy shall follow me all the days of my life; and I will dwell in the house of the Lord forever.
>
> Psalm 23:1–6 NKJV

You may not say "Yay!" when you go through a valley of despair, but you can certainly choose to "fear no evil." You can choose to believe that God "is with me." You can let Him comfort you as He sets a table for you in the midst of your enemies of anxiety, apathy, sadness, loneliness, despair, or depression.

Replacing My Sadness with God's Joy

Joy is much deeper than happiness. Happiness depends on our circumstances. Joy shines in like a ray of light into the darkness of despair. Joy is the truth of who God is. Joy is a settled confidence in the goodness of God. Joy is living in God's presence—fully alive.

As you and I *choose* to live and walk in the presence of God, His joy will win over every dark thought. Joy is not the absence of pain. Jesus himself felt pain on the cross, but Hebrews 12:2 says:

> We do this by keeping our eyes on Jesus, the champion who initiates and perfects our faith. *Because of the joy* awaiting him, he endured the cross, disregarding its shame. Now he is seated in the place of honor beside God's throne.

Jesus knew joy awaited Him. You are destined for that same joy. Deep, satisfying, fulfilling joy designed by God is the culmination of your journey. But you don't have to wait for it. It is also a fuel. Joy neutralizes restless discontent and energizes purposeful pursuit—and it's yours now.

Nothing can steal God's joy. A rainy day does not squelch His delight in you or the world that He made. God does not become concerned with delays or setbacks. He is above time. He lives in eternity. God is not easily hurt. He never becomes offended. God's joy is an eternal peace that consequences or circumstance cannot quench.

The joy of the Lord is the strength of every woman of prayer. You are able to replace your sadness with His joy through spending daily time in conversation with God. Joy is the life-giving, hope-filling, peacemaking presence of God. Our joy is ultimately found in our relationship with God. He is the only One who truly satisfies. He is the One who can make your soul content.

Radical joy is a choice of daily gratitude. Gone are your moments of entitled living. Here to stay is the ever-present reality of God-with-Us—Emmanuel. At Christmas, when we sing "Joy to the World," we are celebrating the triumphant victory of God coming in the flesh. He came down to earth to be one of us. He knows our pain. He suffered and bled and died for us.

Move forward with faith-filled and power-packed celebration of God's joy. Expect His joy in unexpected places and faces. His joy is contagious. It swallows up sorrow and pain with the wonder of who He is.

~PRAY~

Jesus, I come to you in weakness. Life can weigh me down at times, but you are my joy and my strength. I can turn to you when all else fails. I can come to you in sadness, weeping, and crying. You wipe away my tears with your promises. Help me to look up to you,

God. You are my shield of protection. You are my strong tower. You are my hope. Today I choose to surrender my life to you. I put in your hands my daily necessities and needs. I believe you to turn my sorrow into dancing. I take off my heavy coat of dread. I trust you to clothe me with gladness.

Weeping may last during the nighttime, but your joy comes in the morning. I put my hope in you, God. You are my joy and delight. Amen (Psalms 16, 30, 43).

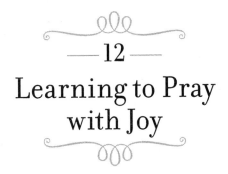

12

Learning to Pray with Joy

Learning to pray with joy often means that you are working through your own sorrow and suffering, trying to give it over to God. Tears can be a sign of God's cleansing presence as you give your pain to Him. Your emotions can ebb and flow, but the truth of God's Word is eternal.

1. Read Philippians 3:1. What are you instructed to do? Why?

2. Read Philippians 3:2–9. What do you learn from Paul's reflections?

3. Read Philippians 3:10–11. How do you suffer with Christ?

4. Read Philippians 3:12–14. How is God speaking to you through these verses?

5. Read Psalm 22:23–25. How does God treat those who suffer? What is our response?

6. Read Psalm 119:71. How does God use suffering in our lives?

7. Read James 5:10–11. What do you learn from the example of Job?

8. Read 2 Corinthians 6:4–10. What do you learn from Paul's suffering?

9. Read 2 Corinthians 7:10–11. What does godly sorrow produce in our lives?

Being Transformed through Prayer

The transformation process in our lives is both instantaneous and ongoing. Our regeneration is a free gift from God. Our discipleship process is a daily choice to obey God and be transformed as we renew our minds by His Word and through prayer.

10. Read Romans 5:6–11. What did Jesus do when we were helpless?

11. Read 2 Corinthians 5:17. What happens when we come to Christ?

12. Read Romans 12:1–2. What does it mean to be a living sacrifice? How does God transform the way we think?

13. Read 2 Corinthians 10:3–5. What is required of us in these verses? How do we take every thought captive and make it obedient to Christ?

14. How does changing the way you think impact how you feel?

Learning from Jesus

Jesus gives us a divine exchange. He suffered and died for our sake so that we can have an eternal future without suffering. He's the One who replaces our sadness with His joy.

15. Read Hebrews 12:1–2. What did Jesus do because of the joy awaiting Him?

16. Read John 16:20–22. What does Jesus promise you in these verses?

17. Read John 17:9–16. What do you learn from Jesus' prayer for us?

18. Read Luke 22:41–43. What do you learn from Jesus' prayer for himself?

19. Read Revelation 21:1–7. What is the promise in your eternal future?

Praying with Confidence, Boldness, and Grace

We have so many examples from giants of the faith on how to pray. When we begin to pray, we may feel overwhelmed, but as we pray our suffering is replaced with His confidence, boldness, and grace. We are empowered to follow Jesus as our prime example when we pray. The Holy Spirit will help us even when we are weak.

20. Read Romans 8:17–25. What do you learn about suffering in these verses?

21. Read Romans 8:26–28. How does the Holy Spirit help in your weakness?

22. Read 2 Corinthians 1:3–7. What does God promise you in these verses?

23. Read James 5:13–16. What do you learn about the power of prayer in these verses?

24. Read James 5:17–18. What do you learn about confidence in prayer from Elijah?

Replacing Sadness with Joy

Sadness and sorrow are a part of the broken condition of humanity.
While we are on this earth we will suffer sickness and setbacks.

The Lies of Sadness

My sorrow will never end.

God causes suffering.

I am not able to control my thought life.

The Truth of Joy

Jesus will wipe away every tear.

Sorrow is our temporary condition.

Joy is our eternal promise.

Learning to Pray with Joy

Joy is a choice to embrace the truth of our eternal promise in the midst of difficult situations. Joy overwhelms sadness little by little. Like the sunshine breaking out after a dreary, rain-soaked day, joy radiates hope. To learn to pray with joy requires you to think positively and choose to receive God's comfort.

25. Write down a timeline of your life. Include the difficult times of suffering that you have experienced. Also include ways that God brought you comfort in the midst of your suffering. You can illustrate your timeline using different colors to represent sadness and joy.

Extending God's Grace

If you don't have a prayer group, grow in your prayer life by gathering women to study and pray together. There is power in united prayer to break the Enemy's attack on our lives. God's grace will be extended to you as you experience His love and acceptance from others in the body of Christ.

For Group Discussion

Bonus Video: Have you ever laughed through your tears? Watch this chapter's bonus video at www.SueDetweiler.com.

26. Share one difficult time in your life. How did the Holy Spirit bring comfort to you? (Be specific.) Are you dealing with sadness or depression right now? How can we pray for you?

— 13 —

I Am Empowered

*Transforming My Perfectionism
by Coming into His Presence*

When my friend Amy Carroll sent me her book *Breaking Up with Perfect*, I couldn't wait to read it. Her call to "kiss perfection goodbye and embrace the joy God has in store for you" really resonates with my heart regarding our call to cultivate God's presence in our life of prayer. I asked Amy to describe a time in her life when she experienced God's presence.

"I was brokenhearted at my broken engagement with the man I thought was the love of my life. I had staked my good-girl-reputation on hearing from God that this was my one-and-only. I was devastated when he broke up with me. I was despondent to the point of being suicidal.

"A week after the breakup, I called my parents and I was sobbing so hard they couldn't understand a word I said. They knew it was me and that I was in pain. At the end of the phone call, my dad asked, 'Amy, you aren't going to hurt yourself, are you?' I responded, 'Well, if a bus came toward me, I wouldn't move out of the way.'

"I had never felt the pain of rejection in such a tangible way. I had come into the relationship feeling the unconditional love that my parents had raised me with. I left deflated and unsure of myself. I didn't know if I could even hear God's voice anymore.

"I went to church and had the pretty plastic smile plastered to my face. I looked like I was doing well. I kept up my perfectionistic charade. But behind the façade, my love relationship with God had gone cold. I wasn't praying. I stopped reading the Bible. I didn't spend time quietly listening for His voice.

"I had not only lost my fiancé, but I had lost communication with the lover of my soul. Six weeks passed, and the tension just increased in my heart and soul. I was alone and abandoned and I was resisting the One who could help me the most.

"One night I was in my apartment by myself. I could hear Jesus calling me to come to Him. His presence was drawing me close. I had avoided His presence by being with friends and reading books. I wanted any story other than the one I was living.

"Jesus, like a patient lover, waited and called. He was calling me to get down on my knees. My perfect life was crumbling. I could no longer pretend that I held it all together. I needed to completely surrender to Jesus.

"I don't know why I waited so long to go to Him. I was afraid that He would be angry with me. I'd failed. I'd held Jesus at arm's length. I was the one who created the distance. I was giving God the silent treatment. But I missed being with Him.

"I finally got on my knees and started crying. I got on my face and sobbed. Rather than an angry response from Jesus, I felt His presence wrap around my whole being. I was washed with His peace. His presence broke me of my need to be perfect. Jesus rescued me from myself and a marriage that would never have worked.

"I came to Him in my imperfection, and I received His perfect love that casts out fear. I poured out my broken heart to Him, and He mended me and set me free. I can truly say that His presence was so real to me in that moment that I tangibly *knew that God was in the room with me.*"

Waving the White Flag

I don't know what it means for you to truly surrender to Jesus. I do know that there are critical moments in each of our lives when we need to wave the white flag and come to our senses. God is able to take our pain, our sorrow, and our imperfections.

Have you been facedown before God? Have you come to the end of yourself, when you knew you couldn't keep up the façade that protected you from harm? We are all tempted to wear masks when we go through difficult things. For Amy, it was a good-girl mask. For others, it can be a rebellious mask. You may have struggled enough in your life that you just stopped trying. You became despondent.

Perfectionism is a blinding foe. You don't realize you have been blindsided until you come to the end of yourself. Perfectionism will drive you to strive for excessively high performance goals. It may cause you to be highly critical. You will be driven to meet impossible standards, unable to please yourself and others. It squeezes the fun out of life and steals the joy out of relationships. Rather than being relaxed and at home with who you are, you may constantly try to be someone else.

Replacing Perfectionism with Presence

Replacing the drive for perfection with the peace-filled presence of the Holy Spirit in your life will rejuvenate you. Learning to relax in God's presence will free you from faultfinding. Perfectionism is a prison that binds you to standards you can never meet. "If you wait for perfect conditions, you will never get anything done" (Ecclesiastes 11:4 TLB).

Perfectionism causes you to hesitate. If you place such high standards on yourself, you will never move forward and obey God. Your internal dialogue could be something like this: *I don't know what to do. I'm afraid that I'm going to get it wrong. I need to just play it safe. If I can't do it perfectly, I won't even try.*

Perfectionism can cause your prayer life to have extreme standards. You may have nagging thoughts or unreal expectations like

If I really knew how to pray, then all my problems would go away. I'm going to set my alarm for 4:00 a.m. and pray for two hours before work. Then when you sleep through your alarm and rush to work, barely getting there on time, you blame yourself for not following through. Any virtue can become a vice when we try to accomplish it in our own strength.

Perfectionism nags at your self-worth and compares you to someone else. You may be your own worst critic when you don't accomplish your goals. The only way to truly overcome perfectionism is through God's grace. His grace sets you free. As human beings, we all fall short of God's standard. That's why we need a Savior.

Coming into God's presence through reading His Word, waiting in prayer, worshiping, and even daily living can erode the perfectionist tendencies in our lives. However, this can be a slippery slope, leaving you feeling pressure to conform to an unattainable goal.

Sustained by His Grace

The key to walking free from perfectionism is being in a personal relationship with Jesus. He said, "Then you will know the truth, and the truth will set you free" (John 8:32 NIV).

He said this to a group of religious leaders who already thought they knew the truth. The Greek word translated know is *ginosko,* which implies a knowledge that is gained from personal experience and relationship.

Legalistic religious requirements can force a type of perfectionistic living that is beyond reach. When these unrealistic standards are pressed, the loving heart of God is missed. Only God is able to see into someone's heart. God always comes with truth and grace at the same time. He draws the sinner home with His love.

In John 8, Jesus confronts the religious leaders of the day. The confrontation begins when the scribes and the Pharisees try to trap Jesus.

Jesus returned to the Mount of Olives, but early the next morning he was back again at the Temple. A crowd soon gathered, and he

129

sat down and taught them. As he was speaking, the teachers of religious law and the Pharisees brought a woman who had been caught in the act of adultery. They put her in front of the crowd.

"Teacher," they said to Jesus, "this woman was caught in the act of adultery. The law of Moses says to stone her. What do you say?"

They were trying to trap him into saying something they could use against him, but Jesus stooped down and wrote in the dust with his finger. They kept demanding an answer, so he stood up again and said, "All right, but let the one who has never sinned throw the first stone!" Then he stooped down again and wrote in the dust.

When the accusers heard this, they slipped away one by one, beginning with the oldest, until only Jesus was left in the middle of the crowd with the woman. Then Jesus stood up again and said to the woman, "Where are your accusers? Didn't even one of them condemn you?"

"No, Lord," she said.

And Jesus said, "Neither do I. Go and sin no more."

John 8:1–11

Every time I read this story I fall in love with Jesus all over again. You may never have been caught in the very act of adultery, but all of us have fallen short of who we are called to be (Romans 3:23). We have also experienced double standards. *Where is the man she was caught in adultery with? Why isn't he on trial?*

Self-righteous men demand that this woman be stoned for her offense. Jesus exposes their hypocrisy with a clear challenge. No one is sinless and able to throw the first stone. When they leave the woman standing alone with Jesus, He challenges her to "go and sin no more." He restores her relationship with God not through legalism, but through grace. How much better for you and me to walk in the beauty of His holiness, sustained by His grace, rather than cajoled by performance. You are holy because of His redemptive grace, not your religious performance.

The religious leaders' treatment of the woman caught in adultery is callous and demeaning. The woman would have been held through the night and in terror as she was publically humiliated in the temple. Her fear of imminent death was likely reflected in her eyes that pleaded for help. In their deceitful legalism, the Pharisees did not care about the emotional state of the woman. They simply wanted to trap Jesus. If He was shown to be lax in following the law, He could be condemned. Their purpose was to use the law to entrap and control.

Jesus was left alone with the woman. He was the only sinless one able to cast the first stone. He could have condemned her, but He chose to call her to a new life. He showed that adultery is a sin and that God mercifully forgives sin when we come to Him. Christ's death atones for all sin. The only sin that will remain unforgiven is the sin we don't repent of.

The men were thwarted in their plan to trap Jesus. They had made a show of following the law of Moses, but their real intent and purpose was to murder Jesus. God, who can see our hearts, knows how to lead us to stand against sin but love and embrace the sinner.

Relationship Rather than Religion

Becoming a woman who moves mountains means that you care more about what Jesus thinks than the Pharisees in your life. Do you have the voice of someone you look up to in your head, telling you to do this or to do that? Perhaps you listen to them talk about their relationship with God and it feels like they are super-Christians. Reject comparisons. Comparing will trap you into religion, not relationship.

The heartbeat of Jesus is available to you as you rest your head on His chest. You can be as close to God as you want to be. You have been promised that if you "draw near to God . . . He will draw near to you" (James 4:8 NKJV).

Have you ever wondered why Jesus always seemed to be fighting with the Pharisees? He was so much harder on them than the "sinners" of the day. In John chapter 8, we learned about the religious leaders who wanted to stone a woman for adultery. Did you notice that at the end of the chapter the religious leaders wanted to stone Jesus?

Religion and rules can lead to hot-headed self-righteousness and hypocrisy in those who appear to be the most devout. Can you imagine praying like this?

> The Pharisee stood by himself and prayed this prayer; "I thank you, God, that I am not like other people—cheaters, sinners, adulterers. I'm certainly not like that tax collector! I fast twice a week, and I give you a tenth of my income."
>
> Luke 18:11–12

This prayer that describes the self-righteous actions of the Pharisee was far from the heart of God. He wasn't praying to God, he was meditating on himself and his own actions. An important part of our prayer life is lining up our heart with the heart of Jesus. Perfectionism can lead us to being proud of what we *accomplish* in prayer rather than what is *accomplished in our hearts*. Jesus pointed out the difference in prayer by calling attention to this:

> But the tax collector stood at a distance and dared not even lift his eyes to heaven as he prayed. Instead, he beat his chest in sorrow, saying, "O God, be merciful to me, for I am a sinner." I tell you, this sinner, not the Pharisee, returned home justified before God. For those who exalt themselves will be humbled, and those who humble themselves will be exalted.
>
> Luke 18:13–14

The tax collector, like the adulterous woman, was a known sinner. Their outward actions were obvious to the Jewish people. But Jesus is calling us to the heart of prayer: humbling ourselves before God. Being justified before God not because of our own actions but because of His mercy. Those who exalt themselves will be humbled, and those who humble themselves will be exalted.

In our worldly system where you "never let them see you sweat," it's all about image and meeting expectations. In Jesus' culture, it's all about humility and building an intimate relationship with God. Jesus was always approachable to sinners.

We All Need Grace

It's a level place at the foot of the cross. We all have a past of sin and regret. We have all lied and done things that we are ashamed of. We all have fallen short of who God has called us to be. When we hear about other people's prayer lives, we just *know* they must be better than ours.

We all need grace. Grace is being free from condemnation, fear, dread, and performance. The standard definition for grace is "unmerited favor," which is so true—we don't deserve it. We can't earn it, but we can receive it. Grace is divine enablement to be who He has made you to be. Grace is breathing room.

Breathe in God's Presence

My daughter Hannah had the word *Breathe* tattooed on her body as a reminder that she can just breathe and it's going to be okay. When Hannah was away for her second year of college, her nineteen-year-old best friend, Beverly, died suddenly. We didn't even know Bev was sick. She had undiagnosed leukemia and died four days before her birthday. She was the person Hannah felt safe with. They were going to be in each other's weddings. Beverly was the person who would say to Hannah, "Just breathe."

Hannah was actually born on the National Day of Prayer, and I named her Hannah for the famous mom of the Bible who cried out to God for a son. Hannah grew up in a home with a mom and dad who were both in ministry. Not only did she sit on the front row every Sunday, she and her sisters were often examples of how you should act in church.

One day when little Hannah and her sisters were sitting on the front row with us, our senior pastor was preaching about the power of prayer. He picked up Hannah and held her up as an illustration that even though Hannah was so tiny, if she prayed in the powerful name of Jesus, she was no longer "Hannah Banana," but she was "Hurricane Hannah." This new nickname stuck, and

Hannah remembered that there is great power when she prays in Jesus' name.

Looking back, I can see how Hannah was constantly pressured to perform. No one had to tell her to spend time in prayer when she went away to college. She would sit in the college lounge every day with her Bible and journal and spend time with God. But even with all these positive Christian habits of prayer, Hannah needs to know and receive God's grace. She does not have to perform. Nor does she have to sit on the front row as an example to everyone. She can just *breathe*.

Prayer is the place where Hannah has been able to be completely vulnerable to God. Losing Beverly was so tough she had to go deeper in her prayer life to survive. She is coming to a place where prayer is like breathing. In the midst of this deeper walk with God, she is being loosed from performance. When Bev died, she knew she couldn't keep it all together. She had to be vulnerable and grieve even if people didn't understand. She knew that God understood. She was learning to breathe.

No Comparisons Needed

We all need grace in the area of prayer. You and I need the clear revelation that Jesus died for us, so we can stop trying to measure up to some invisible standard. We can talk to God anytime, anywhere, and any way that brings life.

Performance breeds fear, dread, anxiety, and sometimes pride. If you are the one with the measuring stick, you may be whacking people on the backside with it, completely unaware that you're doing it. I have been like that. I have gotten up early for prayer. I have prayed in the middle of the night. I have spent hours in Bible study and prayer. I have memorized Scripture. I have led early-morning prayer for decades. I have spent entire days fasting and praying. I have prayed out loud, declaring things over our city. I have held the keys to an executive tower in the city that was rented for the purpose of upper-room prayer meetings. I have led city-wide prayer and have been a part of numerous national prayer movements.

Just like Paul, who cited all of his religious accomplishments, I quickly share these details and call them rubbish compared to the knowledge of the grace of God and walking freely with God, not under the religious law of performance.

Paul said,

> I once thought these things were valuable, but now I consider them worthless because of what Christ has done. Yes, everything else is worthless when compared with the infinite value of knowing Christ Jesus my Lord. For his sake I have discarded everything else, counting it all as garbage, so that I could gain Christ and become one with him. I no longer count on my own righteousness through obeying the law; rather, I become righteous through faith in Christ. For God's way of making us right with himself depends on faith. I want to know Christ and experience the mighty power that raised him from the dead. I want to suffer with him, sharing in his death.
>
> Philippians 3:7–10

Once again, Paul is using the Greek word *ginosko*, which has been translated to "know" Christ. Everything is garbage compared to being in an intimate, loving, merciful, grace-filled, truth-empowering relationship with Jesus Christ.

~PRAY~

Jesus, there is no one who compares to you. Forgive me for trying to perform to please you and others. I know that my human attempts at righteousness cannot take the place of the right relationship you purchased for me on the cross. I cast down my religious pretense.

I lay aside every Christian badge of honor. Instead, I humbly embrace my moment-by-moment need for you. Amen.

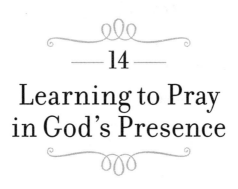

14

Learning to Pray in God's Presence

Overcoming perfectionism in your own life begins when you embrace the only one in your life who is perfect—God! The Father sent His Son, Jesus, to earth. Jesus is the only one who lived a sinless life and died on the cross to free us from sin.

1. Read 1 John 1:8. What does this verse say to you about perfectionism?
2. Read 2 Corinthians 12:9–10. What do you learn from this Scripture?
3. Read 2 Samuel 22:31. How does God's presence protect you?
4. Read Psalm 18:30. What do you learn about God?
5. Read Psalm 18:32. How does God's presence impact the direction you should go?
6. Read Mark 10:27. What is God saying to you in this verse?

Overcoming Christian Perfectionism

I have prayed with many who have struggled with perfectionism in their Christian faith. Because they want to know God's way for their lives, they struggle to know how to perfectly obey Him. At the root of their struggle is a desire not to experience pain, loss, or failure. It's a false American theological view that has made its way into the minds of Christians. The thought process is something like this: *If I hear God perfectly, I will not fail. If I obey God completely, I will not suffer. If I am in the center of God's perfect will, I will not make a mistake.*

7. Have you ever struggled with perfectionism in your thought processes?
8. Does God promise you will not experience pain or suffering in this life?
9. Read Psalm 46:10. What does this Scripture say to you?

Learning to Embrace Who You Are in Christ

The Enemy is like a blowfish. He will try to exaggerate things in your life and lead you to live in extremes. Learning to embrace who you are in Christ requires that you know Christ intimately. One of the ways to know Jesus is to meditate on His Word. The following statements are based on God's Word. Look up each Bible reference noted to learn from the context. Then speak each statement out loud and embrace the good news about who you are in Christ:

I am forgiven (1 John 2:12).
I am a child of God (1 John 3:1–2).
I am a living stone (1 Peter 2:5).
I am blameless and free from accusation (Colossians 1:22).
I am firmly rooted in Christ (Colossians 2:7).
I am chosen (Colossians 3:12).
I am loved (1 John 4:10).
I am Christ's friend (John 15:15).

I am a joint-heir with Christ (Romans 8:17).
I am more than a conqueror (Romans 8:37).
I am called (1 Corinthians 7:17).
I am a new creation (2 Corinthians 5:17).

Praying with Confidence, Boldness, and Grace

We learn from pain, loss, and failure. God uses the difficult things in our lives to make us more like Him. Becoming a woman who moves mountains does not mean that prayer will take you to a realm where you are above experiencing emotional pain and loss. Prayer connects you to the heartbeat of Jesus, who suffered and died for us. Becoming a woman who moves mountains means that you become *better* rather than *bitter* as you go *through* difficulties. The key to going through a crisis is to stay close to Jesus and follow the leading of His Holy Spirit.

Replacing Perfectionism with Presence

Perfectionism drives you to strive in your own strength.
Jesus gives you His strength and ability.
Perfectionism causes strife in your relationships.
The presence of Jesus brings healing to your relationships.

The Lies of Perfectionism

I have to measure up.
I have to perform excellently to be accepted.
If I fail I will be rejected.
I can do it in my own strength and ability.

The Truth of His Presence

God's presence brings peace to your heart and soul.
In God's presence there is fullness of joy in your life.
In God's presence you find healing and hope.
In God's presence your relationships are healed.
In God's presence you are strengthened and
  encouraged.
In God's presence you overcome the Evil One.

Learning to Pray in God's Presence

If you leave your time of prayer more anxious than when you began, you are not praying in God's presence. If your mind is wrought with frustration, you may be tempted to spend your time complaining rather than casting your cares on God. If you leave your prayer time with a whole list of things that you must do in order to please God or curry His favor, you may have been listening to a religious spirit trying to entrap you in perfectionism.

In God's presence you will experience peace, joy, and revelation. You will not feel a soulish urgency to do something, you will sense a calm leading of His Spirit. He may prompt you to do something right away, but it will not carry a frenetic pressure to perform. Instead, you will know that God is leading you and guiding you.

Prayer Journal

Take your journal and Bible and get away from the rush of the day. You may have to plan ahead so that you have time to really listen to God. Begin your time of prayer in worship and thanksgiving. Begin to write in your journal all the things that you are thankful to God for in your life. Then write down in your journal this question: *God, are there areas in my life where I am trying to perform to please you or others?* Then just quiet your mind and listen for the Holy Spirit to answer you. Write down what you sense the Spirit saying. You will notice that His words will fill you with a sense of peace and will line up with His Word.

After you have written down what you believe God has said to you about perfectionism, write down this statement and question in your journal: *I want to hear your voice leading me and guiding me every day. I know that your voice will line up with your Word. Is there anything that you want to say to me today that would help me walk in your presence moment by moment?* Listen to what He says to you and write it down.

Extending God's Grace

Next time you are in a hospital room or with someone who is far away from the Lord's presence, pray for God's presence to come into the room and fill it with His peace.

For Group Discussion

In what ways do you struggle with perfectionism? What perfect expectations of yourself or others do you need to let go of?

Bonus Video: Have you ever been surprised to discover the perfection you were aiming for was all in your own mind? Watch this bonus video at www.SueDetweiler.com.

10. Why is it important for you to relax and come into God's presence? What negative thoughts about yourself do you need to replace with God's Word about who you are in Christ?

15

I Am Humble

Transforming Entitlement into Humility

As an author, speaker, ministry leader, and sexual abuse survivor, Mary Demuth has led the way in helping people deal with their difficult past to become in her words a "forward-momentum person with a story that changes the world." Since I am now a fellow Texan, I reached out to Mary and found out that she had been a church planter in France. Her story challenges all of us who feel like we are entitled to a happily-ever-after success story when we obey God. Here are Mary's words:

"When we came home from France after being church planters there for two and a half years, I received an email from a friend asking me if we'd missed God by going there in the first place. After all, we came home early, so maybe our going had been a failure on our part to hear God's voice in the first place. That would neatly explain why things didn't quite work out as we had planned.

"I prayed, and then spent a lot of time answering my friend. The gist of my communication was this: It's an American idea that if God calls us to a task, and He is truly in it, then success always follows.

"I hate to say this, but it's not always true. In fact, it's seldom true. Dietrich Bonhoeffer wrote this: 'When Christ calls a man, he bids him come and die. It may be a death like that of the first disciples who had to leave home and work to follow him, or it may be a death like Luther's, who had to leave the monastery and go out into the world. But it is the same death every time—death in Jesus Christ, the death of the old man at his call.'[1]

"Following Jesus wherever He leads means walking down frightening paths. It means risk—of reputation, of meeting society's neatly packaged goals, of your own concept of victory. It means thinking beyond your personal kingdom to the kingdom of God.

"We are far too shortsighted if we feel that following Jesus is the pathway to worldly (or even churchly) success. He is the pathway to new life, yes. But new life springs from death.

"When we returned from France, defeated and bone-tired, one of my husband's seminary professors told us: 'Nothing significant in the kingdom happens unless death occurs.' That encouraged us.

"We rested there, hoping and believing that our toil in a foreign land, though not magnanimous or something tangible to point to, meant something in the silent, growing, unseen kingdom. Nearly four years in the aftermath of coming home, we're beginning to see it.

"We're deeper. We have more empathy. We understand many who go through hell in ministry. We can walk alongside those who feel bewildered by their calling. We understand slander, misunderstanding, and shattered dreams. We are weaker, but in that token, we are stronger because Christ's strength is made perfect in weakness (2 Corinthians 12:9–10 NIV).

"We may walk with a limp, not having 'conquered France for Jesus.' But we were faithful there, doing the next thing, then the next thing, then the next thing. We persevered through mounting trials. (After one year on the field, we were both diagnosed with PTSD. Yep, a lot of stress.) We kept the faith. Our children are in love with Jesus.

"Did we miss God by going to France, then coming home early? No. We learned valuable lessons about sacrifice, death, and the beauty of trusting even when the outcome is dark. As my husband said recently to some other former missionaries, 'I firmly believe God sent us to France. And I firmly believe he brought us back to the States.'

"May we believe God is big enough to bring us through perceived ministry failure for the sake of His name, His glory, His plan. May we be humble enough to be small for the kingdom's sake so His story resounds. And when God calls us again to do a difficult task, without promise of tangible, spectacular results, may we plow forward in joyful obedience."[2]

Living Relationship with God

To have a living, vital relationship with God, we die to ourselves. To die to self is to set aside our own wants and desires and focus on loving and serving God. As we die to ourselves, we no longer try to keep up appearances or get our own way. We stop having an I-know-better-than-you mentality. This dying process looks different for each of us and is described by Paul in Galatians 2:

> What actually took place is this: I tried keeping rules and working my head off to please God, and it didn't work. So I quit being a "law man" so that I could be God's man. Christ's life showed me how, and enabled me to do it. I identified myself completely with him. Indeed, I have been crucified with Christ. My ego is no longer central. It is no longer important that I appear righteous before you or have your good opinion, and I am no longer driven to impress God. Christ lives in me. The life you see me living is not "mine," but it is lived by faith in the Son of God, who loved me and gave himself for me. I am not going to go back on that.
>
> Is it not clear to you that to go back to that old rule-keeping, peer-pleasing religion would be an abandonment of everything personal and free in my relationship with God? I refuse to do that,

to repudiate God's grace. If a living relationship with God could come by rule-keeping, then Christ died unnecessarily.

vv. 20–22 MSG

Dying to self means living for Christ. After we go through that dying process, things are actually easier. We don't feel hurt when we are overlooked. We are secure in God's love without the need for public recognition.

There are things in life that we can't make happen no matter how long and hard we pray. We may feel entitled to success because we have been faithful and worked hard. We may pray with so much vigor, we are sure things will turn out the way we hoped.

Dying to self has become less popular in our American culture, where everyone is a winner and no one ever loses. *The Narcissism Epidemic: Living in the Age of Entitlement* describes growing narcissism in today's culture:

> On a reality TV show, a girl planning her sixteenth birthday party wants a major road blocked off so a marching band can precede her grand entrance on a red carpet. A book called *My Beautiful Mommy* explains plastic surgery to young children whose mothers are going under the knife for the trendy "Mommy Makeover." It is now possible to hire fake paparazzi to follow you around snapping your photograph when you go out at night—you can even take home a faux celebrity magazine cover featuring the pictures. A popular song declares with no apparent sarcasm, "I believe that the world should revolve around me!"[3]

The core of narcissism is a grandiose perception of yourself. A narcissist believes that he or she is better than everyone else and deserves special privileges. These beliefs have gone beyond individuals with a narcissistic personality disorder and have become a part of our American culture.

The core of this narcissism epidemic conflicts with and is opposed to fundamental Christian beliefs. Jesus said, "For even the Son of Man did not come to be served, but to serve, and to give

His life a ransom for many" (Mark 10:45 NKJV). He calls His disciples to serve others and says, "If anyone desires to come after Me, let him deny himself, and take up his cross daily, and follow Me" (Luke 9:23 NKJV).

As Christians, we can slip into this culture of entitlement, buying into an individualistic version of following God and fulfilling our destinies. Then if we obey God, we feel like we are guaranteed success.

Miriam's Story: Crossing the Line

I loved reading about Miriam when I was a little girl. When her little brother Moses was put in a basket and floated down the River Nile, Miriam is the one who followed and kept watch. She was bold enough to come forward and talk to Pharaoh's daughter.

When Moses came back after forty years in the desert, Miriam took up a place of leadership alongside her brothers, Moses and Aaron: "For I brought you out of Egypt and redeemed you from slavery. I sent Moses, Aaron, and Miriam to help you" (Micah 6:4).

After Moses stretched out his rod and the mighty power of God parted the Red Sea, it was Miriam who led as a prophet. She led the women in a celebration dance. Miriam's prophetic songs were sung through the generations:

> When Pharaoh's horses, chariots, and charioteers rushed into the sea, the Lord brought the water crashing down on them. But the people of Israel had walked through the middle of the sea on dry ground! Then Miriam the prophet, Aaron's sister, took a tambourine and led all the women as they played their tambourines and danced. And Miriam sang this song: "Sing to the Lord, for he has triumphed gloriously; he has hurled both horse and rider into the sea."
>
> Exodus 15:19–21

Miriam was respected. She led alongside Moses and Aaron. This was a gigantic task that required strength and wisdom. If Miriam's story ended at Exodus 15, we would see only her success.

On the border of the promised land Miriam and Aaron were infected with jealousy and entitlement. Gossiping against Moses, their brother and the leader of the nation, exposed their hearts:

> Miriam and Aaron began to talk against Moses because of his Cushite wife, for he had married a Cushite. "Has the Lord spoken only through Moses?" they asked. "Hasn't he also spoken through us?" And the Lord heard this.
>
> (Now Moses was a very humble man, more humble than anyone else on the face of the earth.)
>
> Numbers 12:1–3 NIV

I think it would be difficult to be the sibling of the humblest man on earth. Miriam and Aaron complained and criticized behind Moses' back. They felt entitled to their prominent roles in leading the nation. Miriam's name is listed first, showing that she was the primary speaker.

In this period of wandering through the wilderness, God was leading the people through the desert with a cloud by day and a pillar of fire at night. If the cloud moved, the people broke up camp and moved with it. Miriam and Aaron were directly confronted by God himself, who saw the motive of their hearts:

> At once the Lord said to Moses, Aaron and Miriam, "Come out to the tent of meeting, all three of you." So the three of them went out. Then the Lord came down in a pillar of cloud; he stood at the entrance to the tent and summoned Aaron and Miriam. When the two of them stepped forward, he said, "Listen to my words: 'When there is a prophet among you, I, the Lord, reveal myself to them in visions, I speak to them in dreams. But this is not true of my servant Moses; he is faithful in all my house. With him I speak face to face, clearly and not in riddles; he sees the form of the Lord. Why then were you not afraid to speak against my

servant Moses?'" The anger of the Lord burned against them, and he left them.

Numbers 12:4–9 NIV

Moses may have felt all alone with leaders on every side challenging his authority. Then his brother and sister stood against his unique role. God is the one who defended Moses' authority through the pillar of the cloud. God claimed that He spoke face-to-face with Moses rather than through dreams and visions.

God's defense of Moses' character and leadership went beyond the words that He spoke to a physical consequence of Miriam and Aaron's sin:

> When the cloud lifted from above the tent, Miriam's skin was leprous—it became as white as snow. Aaron turned toward her and saw that she had a defiling skin disease, and he said to Moses, "Please, my lord, I ask you not to hold against us the sin we have so foolishly committed. Do not let her be like a stillborn infant coming from its mother's womb with its flesh half eaten away."
>
> So Moses cried out to the Lord, "Please, God, heal her!"
>
> The Lord replied to Moses, "If her father had spit in her face, would she not have been in disgrace for seven days? Confine her outside the camp for seven days; after that she can be brought back." So Miriam was confined outside the camp for seven days, and the people did not move on till she was brought back.

Numbers 12:10–15 NIV

Miriam's entitlement cost her the public humiliation of being outside the camp for seven days before being restored to the community. Leprosy was seen not just as a disease that ate away the skin but a picture of the contagious infection of sin.

Miriam, like Moses and Aaron, never entered into the promised land. After this public rebuke there is no record of Miriam holding the same level of authority or leadership. Miriam began triumphant, but faded into dishonor and obscurity.

Pride Is a Secret Enemy

Pride is deceptive. You may have been blindsided by pride like Miriam was. You didn't realize you were walking in entitlement until the ugly sin was out in the open. You may be unaware of your pride, but those closest to you have been impacted by its hot blows.

Pride is the basis of all sin. Pride is the door that allows other sins like anger and rage to make their home in your heart. Pride shows itself in so many ways. Pride blocks your ability to hear God's voice.

Pride precedes prayerlessness. If you feel like you don't need God, you will not pray. Pride blinds you to your own weakness and need for God. Pride exaggerates your own strength. You start to take credit in your life for what God did through you. Pride will lead you further from God. Your prayers will become hollow and you will not have the sweet intimacy with God that comes when you walk in humility. Heaven will become silent to your requests.

If you feel like heaven is silent, you may want to examine your own heart for pride. If you feel like you have accomplished everything in your own strength, you may be walking in pride.

Pride creates strife. If you seriously believe that you are *always* right, you will experience a lot of conflict in your life. I regret the times that I have blamed my husband or my children when my own critical heart was to blame. Pride is the gasoline that turns a disagreement into an all-out war.

Humility Is a Guide for Life

Humility is a guide that leads us to fulfillment in life. Humility leads to honor and favor with God. Walking in humility will lead you to make choices that value relationships. Humility helps you to be the best version of *you* while you help others fulfill God's call on their lives.

God's ways are higher than the world's ways. Our American culture encourages us to strive and succeed. It doesn't seem to matter who you climb over, hurt, and wound as long as you find success. The climb to fame can be littered with immoral choices. The emptiness at the top of fame is strewn with broken relationships.

God promotes and gives grace to the humble, but He frustrates and resists the proud (1 Peter 5:5). God's honor is poured out on those who are not seeking it for themselves. Favor from God increases your ability to help and serve people. Humility casts down pride and pretentiousness and embraces strength under restraint. Meekness of mind and heart fashion a character of submission in prayer.

As Christians we are headed in a different direction than the world is headed. The way up to greater Christian influence is down through sacrificial servanthood. Humility is the result of knowing who we are in Christ. This doesn't mean we have a poor self-image. Humility anchors on God's greatness and majesty. We are made in God's image. If you and I walk in humility, what we do in secret will be rewarded openly.

Humility Helps Us Hear His Voice

God's voice differs from our own. However, when we so badly want our own way, it can be dangerously easy to mistake our thoughts and emotions for God's wisdom. So how do you know the difference? How do you know if God is really speaking to your heart? The answer: God's voice is always consistent with His Word. One guiding Scripture on gaining His wisdom: "But the wisdom that comes from heaven is first of all pure; then peace-loving, considerate, submissive, full of mercy and good fruit, impartial and sincere" (James 3:17 NIV).

Wisdom from God brings peace and assurance to your heart. To hear His voice, you must be willing to submit to Him and surrender to His leading. His voice will be confirmed by the good fruit produced by the Word. When you surrender to wisdom from above that is impartial and sincere, you are able to act with both humility and boldness. His wisdom is so pure and full of mercy that you won't want to fight for your selfish ways.

God's Voice Will Lead You on the Path of Life

It will be difficult to truly hear God's voice if you are focused on getting your own way. Allowing the Holy Spirit to cleanse your heart by reading God's Word and turning away from sin will open the door to greater revelation. You will more readily hear God's voice in prayer if you have determined in advance to yield to God's will. One prayer that I have prayed at pivotal turning points in my life is:

> Lord,
>> I will go anywhere you want me to go.
>> I will say anything you want me to say.
>> I will do anything you want me to do.
>> I will serve who you want me to serve.

This is the prayer that I pray when I don't yet know what God is saying. When your life takes unexpected twists and turns, trusting in God's leading is key. Knowing that He is good will bring peace in times when you are not sure what He is doing.

God's Voice Awakens the Unexpected

After twenty-eight years of pastoral ministry in Nashville, I prayed this prayer, not expecting to be awoken the next day with a vision of the state of Texas outlined in flames. As I saw this vision, I knew that God was outlining new territory for us. As we shared the vision with trusted leaders and prayed, God opened the door for us to plant and pastor Life Bridge Church north of Dallas.

Humble and Bold

Humility and boldness are two sides of our prayer lives. We will talk more about boldness in another chapter, but I mention it here on purpose. Often people get caught in a trap, thinking that to be humble means that you need to be passive. But you and I are called to be humble and bold at the same time. There is a tension in this dynamic paradox between knowing by the Spirit when to bow down on your knees and accept the will of almighty God and when to rise up in bold faith to fight for the fullness of your inheritance. The key to knowing the way you should pray is being in tune with the Spirit of God.

To be humble means that you do not think more highly of yourself than you do of others. You have an accurate view of who God has made you to be. Your bold faith is not founded on a confidence in your own abilities, but on the ability of God to intercede on your behalf:

> Therefore, since we have a great high priest who has ascended into heaven, Jesus the Son of God, let us hold firmly to the faith we profess. For we do not have a high priest who is unable to empathize with our weaknesses, but we have one who has been tempted in every way, just as we are—yet he did not sin. Let us then approach God's throne of grace with confidence, so that we may receive mercy and find grace to help us in our time of need.
>
> Hebrews 4:14–16 NIV

Confidently approach God, knowing that He will help you in your time of need. God sympathizes with our weakness but doesn't leave us there. Our time of need becomes an opportunity to grow and become more like Jesus. Humble faith tenaciously perseveres and holds on to truth. What Jesus did on the cross makes it possible for us to come to God face-to-face. Jesus has made a way for us to confidently approach the Father and receive not only His mercy but His grace.

~PRAY~

Jesus, show me how to pray in each situation. God, I know that there are times that I need to simply surrender and rest in you. Jesus, I want to be more like you. You made yourself of no reputation. You took on the nature of a servant. Your name is above every name. You took the lowest place and gained the most exalted place. Jesus, I confess my sin of pride and give you permission to reveal when I am walking in entitlement. Cleanse me from the narcissistic attitudes of my culture. I am a citizen of heaven first.

Open my eyes to see things the way you see them. Awaken me to your Word, will, and way.

Lead me daily and moment by moment. I want to be in step with you. Amen.

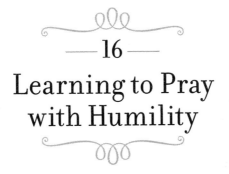

— 16 —

Learning to Pray with Humility

Pride corrupts our perspective and leads us into sin. Sin can beat you down and make you feel powerless to overcome your present circumstance, or it can puff you up and make you feel like you don't need God. God's Word empowers you to be all that God means you to be as you serve others. Learning to pray with humility requires each of us to search our heart and motives as we pray.

1. Read Proverbs 11:12. What is God saying to you in this verse?
2. Read Proverbs 16:18. How have you personally experienced the truth of this verse?
3. Read Proverbs 22:4. What did you learn from this verse?
4. Read James 4:1–3. What is the Lord saying to you in these verses?
5. Read James 4:4–5. List any areas in your life where you have befriended the world.

6. Read James 4:6. Who does God oppose? Have you ever experienced His opposition in your life?

7. Read James 4:7–9. List the step-by-step process of coming closer to God.

8. Read James 4:10. What does the Lord promise if you walk through His process?

9. Read James 5:13–14. What action are you to take if you are going through difficulties?

10. Read James 5:15–16a. What action are you to take if you are dealing with sickness?

11. Read James 5:16b–18. What examples of power-packed prayers are given in these verses?

12. As you have prayerfully read through these verses in the book of James, what is God saying to you about the power of prayer?

Praying with Confidence, Boldness, and Grace

Layer by layer your pride can be replaced with His purity. You may have already experienced great freedom from sin in your life, yet freedom is like an onion. Every new season of life you experience new difficulties where you need His purifying process to bring you close to His heart. With every layer of this freedom process there may be fresh revelation. Think of an area in your life where the finger of God is calling you to walk free from pride. Expect His grace to meet you in this process.

13. Read Ephesians 4:31. Acknowledge the pain and the sin. Often the root of sin is not only pride but also the pain you have experienced. Write down a negative pattern in your life that you want to get rid of.

14. Read Ephesians 4:32. Sit quietly before God and let His Spirit soften your heart. Ask God to show you a relationship that is filled with strife. Take time to write down your forgiveness of the one who has hurt you. The one you need to forgive could

even be yourself. Ask God to show you if there is anything
you can do to mend the relationship.

15. Read Lamentations 3:22–23. Receive Jesus' love and mercy.
    What promise does God give in this Scripture?

Replacing Entitlement with Humility

The American culture has produced an idol of self.
The culture of entitlement has seeped into the church.
Pride in self and accomplishments produces prayerlessness.

The Lies of Entitlement

I need to protect my rights.
I deserve to get my own way.
I am right all the time.

The Truth of Humility

Humility has a sober view of self and others.
Humility is the foundation of virtue.
Humility leads to honor, favor, and intimacy
with God.

Learning to Pray with Humility

Power-packed prayer is not based on how loud you scream at the
devil. Power in earnest, heartfelt prayer comes from God himself, who
backs up your prayer with His answer. Humble yourself before God
and He will not only lift you up, He will hold you up (see James 4:10).

16. Turn to a fresh journal page and write: "God, show me areas
    in my life where I have felt entitled to positions, things, or

relationships." Then wait on God and listen to His voice and write down the list He shows you.

17. On the next journal page write: "God, I know that you resist the proud. Show me areas in my life where I have been proud." Listen and write down what you hear the Holy Spirit saying to you.

18. On the next journal page write: "God, I choose to repent and turn away from every form of entitlement and pride. Holy Spirit, I know that you do not condemn me or put me down, but you convict me of sin. I give you permission to convict my heart when I am walking in pride. Place on me the apron of a servant. Help me to follow hard after you with both humility and boldness." Continue writing your prayer to God as the Spirit leads you.

Extending God's Grace

If you don't have a prayer group, grow in your prayer life by gathering a group of women to study and pray together. There is power in united prayer to break the Enemy's attack on our lives. God's grace will be extended to you as you experience His love and acceptance from others in the body of Christ.

For Group Discussion

Bonus Video: Have you ever been caught with your hand in the cookie jar? In this chapter's video, we take a closer look at how entitlement sneaks into our lives without our recognizing it. Watch this bonus video at www.SueDetweiler.com.

19. How have you seen entitlement manifested in today's culture? It can be difficult to see our own pride. Talk about what the Holy Spirit showed you as you wrote in your journal. In what ways can we pray for you right now?

17

I Am Bold

Transforming Timidity into Boldness

"I was painfully shy and afraid of people. I never wanted to draw attention to myself. I tried to dress like everyone else and have everything in order. My school uniform was spick-and-span and I didn't have a hair out of place. I wanted to disappear so that I would be invisible."

My friend Ann Anderson is a successful business owner and leader of the Women Enhancing Business group at the Frisco, Texas, Chamber of Commerce. Ann is well liked and an influencer of women. I was surprised when she shared with me her battle to overcome timidity in her life.

"I could hardly make myself go to the grocery store when I was newly married. There were so many choices I would have to make and I was afraid to ask questions. I didn't want to stand out. I was paralyzed.

"It was my husband, Thor, who was constantly pushing me out of my comfort zone. He would pull me into the grocery store that I was so afraid of and dance with me in the aisles. Here I was, afraid to be seen and making a scene dancing the waltz on aisle 11.

"Thor would say, 'Of course you will get that promotion,' and then push me out the door to get to the airport. I had to learn to walk through the airport alone and get on the plane. My weight was a real issue for me. I was 280 pounds and I could barely buckle the seatbelt on the airplane. I knew I had to do something, but felt powerless to change.

"I began to quote out loud: 'For God has not given us a spirit of fear and timidity, but of power, love, and self-discipline' (2 Timothy 1:7).

"I needed to remind myself that God loved me and that I was worthy. I was fighting through so much insecurity.

"I would stand outside of an office that I needed to walk into to do my job and say, 'God, please help me. I need to walk through that door.' The scariest part was opening the door. As I grew in my relationship with God, He spoke to my heart. By holding myself back, I wouldn't become the person that He created me to be. So I forced myself to get out of my comfort zone.

"I had a horrible back injury that forced me to take stock of my life. I had back surgery with a long recovery, where I couldn't do anything. I found myself praying a lot those days. For me, prayer is like a constant conversation that never ends.

"My injury and the medicine I took for it made me continue to gain weight. I wore black or dark blue all the time to try to hide how heavy I was. When I was challenged to work out, I didn't even know if I had sweat pants that would fit me, I was so big. I began the journey of weight loss at the same time a change was coming in my work.

"I could tell that a transition was coming. When I had the opportunity to begin my own business, it took me three weeks to make the decision. As we prayed together as a couple, Thor and I sensed God calling us to take the risk.

"Beginning my own business didn't just mean that I was taking a risk financially. I needed to get myself out in the public and build relationships. I had to listen and be in tune with God's voice to help me through it.

"It's scary to walk into a room and be bold enough to stretch out your hand and make a connection. I had to remind myself that the Spirit of God dwells in me. 'If God is for me, who can be against me?' (see Romans 8:31).

"I would tell myself, 'If you can stand up and walk across the room, it will be better than you can imagine.' I needed God to help me walk across the room. When I obeyed, I found contentment in being in God's will.

"You will have to find courage and boldness to fulfill God's call on your life. As I began to get busier in work, Thor challenged me to begin to work out at 5:30 in the morning before my workday. I said, 'Well, if God wakes me up that early, I'll go.' Of course, God woke me up and I had to go.

"Day after day of working out and eating right made me begin to feel healthier. As I became healthier, I had energy to work out. When I began to fit into my clothes, I didn't feel so out of place. I didn't take a pill or follow a magic diet. It was getting up every day and deciding to be healthier.

"I needed to put God first and follow Him faithfully. He's the One in charge of my business and my life. I have met the most amazing people in the last three years. God has helped me to overcome my timidity and walk boldly and confidently into my future. I haven't arrived, but I am enjoying the journey of walking with God and obeying Him."

Transforming Timidity into Boldness

Timidity is not only being shy, it also has to do with a tendency to draw back and hesitate. The key Scripture that Ann meditated on has helped so many people find freedom from timidity:

For God did not give us a spirit of timidity or cowardice or fear, but [He has given us a spirit] of power and of love and of sound judgment and personal discipline [abilities that result in a calm, well-balanced mind and self-control].

2 Timothy 1:7 AMP

The Amplified version explains that timidity is cowardice or fear. Ironically, timidity can be a type of pride as well. When we care more about what people think about us than how God thinks of us, our timidity becomes a preoccupation with self.

God has given us power, love, sound judgment, and self-discipline. We become bold and fearless when we are not afraid of what could happen to us. We are focused and committed to following the leading of the Holy Spirit rather than concerned with our self-image. Boldness leads to an adventurous, audacious faith that doesn't back down from conviction.

Bold Faith

Jesus rewarded bold faith. When He walked on this earth, He responded to the faith of others. He was never too busy to be available to minister to people's needs. One day, He met a prominent leader of the Galilee synagogue:

> After Jesus crossed over by boat, a large crowd met him at the seaside. One of the meeting-place leaders named Jairus came. When he saw Jesus, he fell to his knees, beside himself as he begged, "My dear daughter is at death's door. Come and lay hands on her so she will get well and live." Jesus went with him, the whole crowd tagging along, pushing and jostling him.

Mark 5:21–24 MSG

Many Jewish leaders of the day were angry with Jesus, but Jairus was desperate. He didn't care about protocol or public opinion. He was determined to save his daughter. As a leader of the synagogue in Galilee, Jairus was well respected. The synagogue was a place where people from the local community came to worship and study Scripture. A ruler of the synagogue would not only have taken care of the building, he would have been in charge of the order of the service. Jairus knew Jesus was the only one who could help him. So together they made their way through the jostling crowd, when Jesus was interrupted:

> A woman who had suffered a condition of hemorrhaging for twelve years—a long succession of physicians had treated her, and treated her badly, taking all her money and leaving her worse off than before—had heard about Jesus. She slipped in from behind and touched his robe. She was thinking to herself, "If I can put a finger on his robe, I can get well." The moment she did it, the flow of blood dried up. She could feel the change and knew her plague was over and done with.
>
> vv. 25–29 MSG

Like Jairus, the woman was desperate. She'd had a continuous hemorrhage for twelve years. The Old Testament Law forbade the woman to go out in public. Since she was considered unclean, everyone she touched would become unclean. Jesus reversed the curse of the law. He had the power of God to heal, transform, and restore the woman from the years of suffering and isolation. She had already tried everything, but the doctors of the day were unable or unwilling to help her. They took her money, but she continued to bleed.

The woman focused her faith on touching Jesus. She knew the Pharisees would condemn her for being in public. She knew the Law. If she touched a rabbi, she would make him unclean. But Jesus was different. She knew that all she had to do was touch the hem of His garment and she would be healed. She struggled and strained through the crowd and at last touched Him:

> At the same moment, Jesus felt energy discharging from him. He turned around to the crowd and asked, "Who touched my robe?"
>
> His disciples said, "What are you talking about? With this crowd pushing and jostling you, you're asking, 'Who touched me?' Dozens have touched you!"
>
> vv. 30–31 MSG

Jesus carried the healing presence of the Holy Spirit. He was so in tune that He sensed the healing power going out from Him and immediately stopped to minister to the one who had risked all to touch Him. The disciples were concerned about going to the next place, while Jesus was available every moment He was on the earth. Jesus didn't worry about the disciples; He stopped to look for the one who had touched His robe:

> But he went on asking, looking around to see who had done it. The woman, knowing what had happened, knowing she was the one, stepped up in fear and trembling, knelt before him, and gave him the whole story.
>
> Jesus said to her, "Daughter, you took a risk of faith, and now you're healed and whole. Live well, live blessed! Be healed of your plague."
>
> vv. 32–34 MSG

Jesus knew that the woman not only had a physical need for healing, but also a social and emotional need to be totally restored. He went deeper, crashing through the twelve years of oppression with a single moment of redemption.

The woman had begun with trembling, but pushed past her fears to boldly reach out and touch the hem of Jesus' robe. She risked it all. Did you notice how Jesus responded to her boldness? He commended her faith and healed her body, mind, soul, and spirit. He went deep into the place of pain for this woman and repaired the breach she had with the community of faith. In one moment, Jesus replaced her shame and timidity with the honor of being made completely whole.

The Touch of Jesus

I don't know the hidden plague that you fight through. I don't know the hidden physical, social, and spiritual needs of your life. However, I have walked with people long enough to know that we all have those areas where we need the touch of Jesus to set us free.

When you are tempted to get stuck in your past and draw back, follow the woman's example and press toward Jesus. Risk it all. Jesus can be trusted with your deepest places of pain. Prayer is deeper than the words we speak. Prayer includes the internal struggle of our soul to break through and find healing and restoration with Jesus.

Boldness helps you to press beyond the norms and expectations of our culture. Being obedient to the call of God on your life will demand, at some point, that you are audacious, dauntless, and relentless in your pursuit of His help. No one is courageous in their own strength. True courage comes from God.

You are transformed as you take steps of faith. You become fearless when you keep your eyes on Jesus. The things that used to frighten you will no longer cause you to hesitate and draw back. Concentrate on God's availability to minister to your need. It is His Spirit alive in you that makes it possible for you to walk in boldness. Facing your fear will free you to see God's power at work in your life.

Shake yourself awake. Shake off your excuses. Do what God is calling you to. Do it afraid, if necessary. Just get moving. He takes the mess of your life and weaves His message into it, but you have to take action.

Bold prayer releases the promises of God in your life. I have found that there are times to wait in peace to receive God's blessings. There are other times that I have to move forward with great effort and lay hold of what He has promised. I have to move forward and not hesitate.

In prayer, I have found this Scripture helpful: "The kingdom of heaven suffers violent assault, and violent men seize it by force [as a precious prize]" (Matthew 11:12 AMP).

The things in your life that you need may come to you with the simplicity of God's faithfulness. However, the things that you really want, that are connected to your destiny, will require you to expend great energy, focus, and risk to seize. Like the woman who was going against all the cultural norms of the day to touch the hem of His garment, you will need to press through your fears with bold faith.

Jesus did not promise us that we would have no fear in this life. Rather, He challenged us to take heart and overcome our timidity with faith and boldness. Jesus said that we would experience trials and stress. We are able to overcome because He overcame. Jesus said, "These things I have spoken to you, that in Me you may have peace. In the world you will have tribulation; but be of good cheer, I have overcome the world" (John 16:33 NKJV).

You and I are not promised a pain-free existence, but we are promised an overcoming life. In the very difficult things that you struggle and strain to overcome, He meets you with His power. Time after time in my own dark hour of the soul, when life looks pitch black, a hymn of hope will rise up in my heart and come out of my mouth in the song "Great Is Thy Faithfulness."

God sees me in the middle of the night, tears dripping down my face, quietly singing, "Great is Thy faithfulness." He hears me in the morning light standing with my face lifted to heaven singing, "Great is Thy faithfulness." He intimately connects with me as I load the dishwasher and wipe the counters singing in my heart, "Great is Thy faithfulness." Our life of prayer is deeper than spoken words and needs to be released as we sing our worship to God.

God's faithfulness penetrates the cold, deathlike grip of fear. His faithfulness transforms perspective. His faithfulness shoots courage into my veins, making it possible to more than just survive a dreaded day. In this world you will face terrible things. You will experience excruciating pain. Fear is a given in this world. The final promise of eternity will outlast all of our fears: "He will wipe every tear from their eyes, and there will be no more death or sorrow or crying or pain. All these things are gone forever" (Revelation 21:4).

Hope stirs my faith when I remember that in the end we win, because He won on the cross. Every tear that I weep as I am crying out for His help is recorded in heaven's books. The injustices that we suffer through in this life are exchanged for His justice in eternity. In this life, God will use the things that you and I have walked through to impact others.

God Sets the Captives Free

We have all been imprisoned by secret areas in our lives. It's a level place at the foot of the cross. Whether you are a murderer, a molester, a thief, or a mom at home impatient with her children, all of us have sinned and fallen short of God's best for our lives (Romans 3:23). All of us need His keys to set us free.

When we hold His keys in our hands, we have bold access to His preferred future for our lives. Jesus had all authority in heaven and on earth and He gave it to us (Matthew 28:18–20). He commissioned us to walk in His authority and make disciples. He set us free to be freedom fighters for others. We can boldly walk like Jesus walked. He gave us these keys to release the captives, and set the oppressed free (Luke 4:18–19).

One day I was walking and praying on a path near our home. I was deep in prayer when I had a vivid picture come to my mind. I saw people behind bars in a jail cell. Some of the people were standing up grasping the bars and trying to shake themselves free. Others were pacing back and forth. Still others were slumped down sitting on a stool. They had given up. They were no longer trying to get free. They had resolved in their minds that they would always be stuck in that dark prison.

When I looked closer at this picture, I realized that each person in the cell already had keys hanging around their neck. One key said *faith* and the other key said *obedience*. I pictured one of the prisoners placing both keys into the locks on the prison door. Suddenly there was an explosion. Their prison bars blew open and were instantly transformed into the railings on a bridge.

As I turned the corner on the walking path, I saw a bridge with railings on it. It was a powerful moment. I felt like God was saying to me: *The very bars in your life that have bound you in the past will become the rails of a bridge to breakthrough.* He showed me that the foundation of the bridge was *faith* and *obedience.* I walked across that bridge and found freedom in Christ.

Jesus is the *Life Bridge.* There is an incredible gap that could not be bridged without Jesus' laying down His life for us. Because He laid down His life for us, we are able to cross over to the other side. In the same way, we lay down our lives for others, and they are able to find freedom in Christ.

Each one of us needs to boldly take His keys in our hand and with faith-filled, obedient hearts break out of our places of captivity. In what area of your life do you need to take action right now? Have you become passive in an area and given up? It will take boldness to overcome things that have bound you in the past.

Your Life Matters

Sometimes the struggles that we face seem insurmountable and we begin to give up. We slump down and give in to the pressures at home and at work. We give in to the temptations of our flesh. We lower our expectations in life because we don't want to be disappointed. We lose our youthful zeal for God and settle for mediocre.

If that's you, you need to shake off your complacency. Your life matters. The freedom you find in Christ will help those who follow after you. The struggle is worth it. It is not in vain.

To be bold is to not hesitate. Boldness overcomes fear in the face of danger. You may have to break the rules of propriety in order to become a hero of faith. Boldness stands up and fights when fear cowers and hides. To be bold means that you will stand out rather than try to fit in.

It is sometimes difficult for women to walk in boldness. As women we often wait for someone to give us permission. We don't want to be perceived as pushy, and we want to walk in submission to God and our leaders. The Enemy knows this and wants to keep our unique contribution to the world hidden with hesitancy and timidity.

Timidity is comfortable when you hide in mediocrity. But God didn't make you to be mediocre. He made you to boldly overcome. The difference between a *victor* and a *victim* is that a victim gives in to the circumstance. A victor *overcomes* the adversity and makes it into an *opportunity* to serve others.

Boldly believe that you can overcome. The keys to becoming a victor have already been given to you because of what Jesus did on the cross. Put the keys of *faith* and *obedience* into the lock of your life, and see the power of God transform the bars that once held you into a *bridge of breakthrough*.

As a woman, you can play the part of the heroine in the story. Yes, it's true. We like to be the fair maiden who is rescued. Yet when we realize that Jesus already rescued us and that He gave us keys to rescue others, we will stop hesitating and waiting for others to answer God's call.

Stand up and fight. You have a unique call of God on your life that is worth fighting for. It will require you to be boldly obedient to God's higher call and let fear and timidity fall to the ground under your feet.

～PRAY～

Jesus, I am answering your call today. I am tired of letting my fear trap me in hesitancy. I repent of my complacency and choose to take action. Jesus, I want your mission to be my mission. Your Spirit, Lord, is already on me. You have anointed me to speak good news to the poor. You have sent me with keys to set free the captives (Luke 4:18).

Make me bold like you. I will lay my hands on the sick and see them recover. I will heal the eyes of the blind so they can see. With your help I will help the oppressed go free.

Lord, your favor is on me for a reason. The favor you have given me is to help others.

Give me your compassion for the burdened. Help me to be sensitive to those tugging on my shirt sleeve. Cause me to notice the one in the jostling crowd that you have sent me to set free. It's by your power and authority that I am a ministry agent of change in people's lives. I embrace your call; I am available for your assignment. Mold me. Use me. Fill me. I cast off my hesitant, timid cloak of complacency. I put on the apron of humility and boldness, ready to serve everyone you send me. In Jesus' name I pray expectantly. Amen.

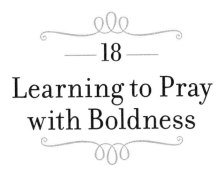

18

Learning to Pray with Boldness

God is generous. He didn't hold back His only Son. He gave Him to die in our place. We can trust Him to provide all we need—both physically and spiritually. When we seek first God's kingdom in prayer, He will add all the elements of our lives that we need. When we chase after God, He gives us the desires of our hearts. God is our provider. He provides one day at a time. We trust Him day by day.

Prayer is not a duty. It is a privilege. It is an honor. We are lifted up to partner with the purposes of God here on earth in prayer. You need to believe that God hears you. You may not get results immediately, but He will go to work on your behalf when you pray.

Jesus pointed to the reality of heaven when He developed a model for prayer. Jesus called us to boldness in prayer. He modeled seeking the Father's will every moment of every day. He called each of us to what is known as the Lord's Prayer.

1. Read Matthew 6:9–13. Write down the Lord's Prayer and memorize it.
2. What does it mean to hallow God's name?
3. How do you bring God's kingdom to earth?
4. What is significant about asking God to give us our daily bread?

5. Why does Jesus include forgiveness in this model for prayer?
6. How do you overcome temptation?
7. What does it mean to give God glory?

Reflections on the Lord's Prayer

When we pray for the will of God to be done, it is not always easy. It is not easy to forgive, but it will change your life and set you free. Jesus included forgiveness in the Lord's Prayer because He knew we couldn't live a holy life without regularly cleansing our spirits with forgiveness. You can't help the way you feel, but you can make a decision to forgive. Sometimes you need to bury your face in the carpet until you choose to love and forgive those who have hurt you. I don't know what vice you struggle with, but I do know who overcame temptation so that you could be free. The Lord's Prayer is a prayer we need to pray every day.

We hallow God's name when we pray according to His character as revealed by His name. Throughout the Old and New Testaments there is a progressive revelation about who He is through the revelation of His name. He is our sanctifier—we have been set apart for His use. Knowing that He has overcome sin and temptation brings new confidence that He will help you to overcome. As you pray, you come into agreement with God's will in heaven and pray for it to become visible here on earth.

Understanding God's Character When You Pray

All human beings (except Jesus) fall short of God's original plan for a perfect world. God has invited us into intimate relationship with Him, which leads to power-packed prayer. You and I have authority to pray in Jesus' name because of what He did on the cross. All the way through the Old Testament God revealed His character by giving us His name. When God appeared to Moses in the burning bush, Moses asked for His name: "And God said to Moses, 'I AM

WHO I AM.' And He said, 'Thus you shall say to the children of Israel, "I AM has sent me to you"'" (Exodus 3:14 NKJV).

This covenant name for God translated I AM WHO I AM is represented by the four Hebrew letters *YHWH*. No one knows exactly how it is pronounced. The Jewish leaders began to regard the personal name of God as too sacred to speak in public. This holy name filled them with awe. As they copied the Old Testament, they would stop, take off their clothes, take a complete bath, put on new clothes, and then copy the name. Today most scholars pronounce God's personal name as Yahweh (Yaaway).

When Jesus died on the cross, the curtain that separated people from the holy of holies in the temple was torn from top to bottom. Jesus made it possible for you and me to come close to God the Father. When Jesus taught His disciples to *hallow God's name*, they already had an understanding of the Hebrew names for God. Take time to meditate on the following names for God as you look up each Scripture reference:

8. Read Jeremiah 23:6. He is our righteousness (Yahweh-Tisdkenu).
9. Read Leviticus 20:8. He is our sanctifier (holiness) (Yahweh-M'Kaddesh).
10. Read Judges 6:24. He is our peace (Yahweh-Shalom).
11. Read Exodus 15:26. He is our healer (Yahweh-Rophe).
12. Read Genesis 22:14. He is our provider (Yahweh-Jireh).
13. Read Exodus 17:15. He is our success (banner) (Yahweh-Nissi).
14. Read Psalm 23:1. He is our guide (shepherd) (Yahweh-Rohi).

Praying with Confidence, Boldness, and Grace

Praying God's Word brings confidence that you are praying in agreement with God's will. To pray God's Word simply means that your prayers are filled with words from Scripture. Scripture prayers help you meditate on God's Word as it comes out of your mouth in the form of a prayer.

Bold, faith-filled prayers are anchored in God's Word. Power-packed prayer is not based on how loud you scream at the devil. Power in earnest, heartfelt prayer comes from God himself, who backs up your prayer with His answer. For example, when you read about the armor of God in Ephesians 6, you can turn this Scripture into a prayer. Let's study the armor of God found in Ephesians 6:10–18:

15. Read Ephesians 6:10–11. Why are you instructed to put on the whole armor of God?
16. Read Ephesians 6:12. Who are we fighting against?
17. Read Ephesians 6:13. How will putting on every piece of armor help you?
18. Read Ephesians 6:14. What two pieces of armor are you instructed to put on? How do these pieces of armor protect you?
19. Read Ephesians 6:15. How does this piece of armor help you?
20. Read Ephesians 6:16. How does this piece of armor protect you?
21. Read Ephesians 6:17. What do you learn from this verse?
22. Read Ephesians 6:18. How does this encourage you to pray?

As you have read about each piece of the armor, it's helpful to understand that Paul was describing the armor used by the Roman soldiers of the day. The helmet would cover the entire head and go over the ears. The breastplate would cover the chest and the heart. The belt would hold everything together. The shoes had nails on the soles and were made to move forward steadily, taking ground and annihilating everything underneath them. The shield was made of metal and covered with soaked leather that instantly extinguished the fiery darts of the enemy. The soldier had two types of swords. The small dagger listed here was used for hand-to-hand combat and could disembowel the enemy. It was also used after battle to dig out tips of arrows that may have embedded in the armor or the flesh of a soldier.

The principal thing to remember is that we are called to fight a spiritual battle through prayer. The Word of God is our main piece of battle equipment. We stand strong when we fight with the power of His Word in prayer.

Now let's put Ephesians 6:10–18 into a prayer that you can pray out loud:

God, you call me to be strong. You equip me with your mighty power. In obedience to your Word, I choose to put on all of your armor so that I am able to stand firm against all the strategies of the devil. I know that we are not fighting against flesh-and-blood enemies. Clothe me in power as I fight against the evil in the unseen world through the power of prayer.

As I put on every piece of your armor, I choose to resist the Enemy in the time of evil. I stand my ground in prayer, putting on the belt of truth and the breastplate of your righteousness. For shoes, I put on peace and open my life to carry the good news wherever you lead me today. I pick up the shield of faith to stop every fiery dart that the devil may shoot my way. I put on the helmet of salvation to protect my mind, and pick up the sword of the Spirit, which is your Word.

Today, I choose to pray in the Spirit at all times and on every occasion. Keep me alert and persistent in my prayers not only for myself, but for believers everywhere. Jesus, thank you for protecting me with your armor today. I pray this in your name, amen.

This is an example of how you can take Scripture that is alive in your heart and turn it into prayer. As you pray God's Word, you will be filled with boldness that comes from His throne of grace.

Replacing Timidity with Boldness

Timidity causes you to hesitate and hold back. Boldness propels you to move forward and take ground. You move forward in your prayer life when you replace timidity with boldness.

The Lies of Timidity

It's wrong to draw attention to myself.

If I try I will fail.

If I step out, I will make a fool of myself.

It's better to be quiet and let others do it.

The Truth of Boldness

Boldness is not hesitant or fearful in the face of danger.

Boldness empowers courage to take ground.

Boldness is needed to fulfill destiny.

Boldness inspires fearless adventure.

Extending God's Grace

Share with a friend a time when you felt timid but God led you to step out in faith and be bold.

For Group Discussion

Bonus Video: Putting on the whole armor of God, as we go into prayer, makes us bold. Once I realized I was in a battle without my armor. Watch this bonus video at www.SueDetweiler.com.

23. There is a spiritual struggle you must go through in prayer in order to fulfill God's call on your life. How has the Lord's Prayer been a guide to you in your prayer life? How does understanding the armor of God help you to be strong in the Lord? How can we pray for you this week?

—19—
I Am Expectant

Transforming Disappointment
and Loss into Hope

"My friend Cristal started rambling on the phone from the moment I said hello. I was lost. I had no idea what she was talking about. Then came the words every mother dreads: *terrible accident, airlifted.* The only thing I fully understood at that moment was that my middle son, Tommy, who was sixteen at the time, was driving and had been in an accident—and I had to get to him."

Before that fateful day, my friend Rhonda's life was pleasantly chaotic as a homeschooling mom of nine children. Her husband, Mike, was well known as a local police officer. Rhonda was a popular columnist for their local newspaper. She wrote about raising a large family in the middle of Illinois's cornfields. As founding members of a local church, their family roots went deep into the soil of their rural community.

Their daughter Hannah was having surgery that morning. With Hannah's fiancé, Mike and Rhonda had traveled about an hour away from home for the procedure. They were scheduled to stay overnight. But all that changed with the phone call.

"A chaplain met us as we rushed into the hospital. Before he would let us see our boy, he ushered my husband and me to a small private room and shut the door. It wasn't until then that I learned the whole truth. My sons Tom and Dan, along with their closest friends, were going to a basketball open gym at a local Christian school. At an unmarked country crossroad, a large pickup truck T-boned the boys' vehicle. That's when the chaplain uttered the most horrific words in the human vocabulary: 'Dan died at the scene.'

"It was instant agony. It felt as if my life was draining out onto the hospital floor, bleeding my soul dry.

"We were blessed to be surrounded by people who wanted nothing more than to love and help us. But as time wore on, everyone went back to their own lives—as they should. But nothing was the same for us. Soon, so much of what had been comforting about the home and community we loved became a trigger for grief. Every time I mustered up the strength to leave the house for something as simple as going to the grocery store, the post office, or the bank, I would see someone who would ask how I was doing. All I wanted was to be invisible.

"After a few months, we started feeling the pressure to resume normal life. Life goes on, they say. But normal would include my Danny.

"We were so devastated by his loss that our lives were broken, and I couldn't fix it. Not for me, not for my children. Our house that had been so full of laughter had turned into a house of sorrow.

"How do you pray when you go through something like this? *Worship.* I found songs that expressed my heart. I became determined to praise God through the storm. Honestly, I never got angry with God, but I struggled to make sense of my own life. Before the accident, everything in my life fit together—I had purpose. After the accident it was hard to find meaning and purpose.

"One of my first turning points came while I was pouring my heart out in prayer. I told God I couldn't do it. It was too hard. I wanted my boy back. I felt God speak to my heart. He said, '*Do you want me to remove him from my presence and give him back to you?'* I knew at that moment that if I loved Danny, I wouldn't take him from the beauty and peace of heaven. It was then I realized that my torn mother's heart needed healing. That not only did I want to keep him in the presence of God, but I needed to make sure all my children would one day join him.

"My prayer life completely changed a few weeks later. As I was praying through tears, again telling God how badly I hurt, I felt Jesus say to my heart, *'Okay, what if I'd said, "Here's the deal: I will give you this handsome, loving boy for thirteen years. No more. After those years, you will mourn for him the rest of your life." Would you have taken him?'* You know what? I would have. Without hesitation—knowing the pain and the joy both having him and losing him would bring. Once I saw it that way, I could focus on being truly thankful for the thirteen years I'd had with him.

"I no longer made demands of God. Instead, I envisioned myself crawling up onto His lap and spilling my tears there. When I hurt the worst, I would sing praises to my Father and thank Him for His mercies. Those two acts of prayer brought peace in the midst of unspeakable sorrow. Life no longer holds guarantees. God is the One who is writing my story. I don't try to take His pen anymore. No matter how it turns out, I can control this: My life will be filled with praise and thankfulness."

God Is Writing Your Story

I don't know what type of pain and loss you have experienced in your past, or will experience in your future. Trauma in our lives dictates a need for recovery. One of the things that plagues our human condition is that we are not able to turn back the clock and recapture yesterday. I resonate with Rhonda's comment that it was impossible to go back to *normal*. When things are broken in our lives, we may want to go backward, but life demands that we go forward.

God is writing your story. He is a redeemer. He will take the pain, sorrow, and loss and use it to make you more like Him. He uses suffering to teach us more about His ways, which are so much higher than our ways.

I am moved by Rhonda's personal determination that no matter what, she would praise God. Life does not hold guarantees for any of us. You can't control your life. Jesus is the only one who is "the same yesterday, today, and forever" (Hebrews 13:8). He is the one who anchors our souls when life is spinning out of control.

Like clay on a potter's wheel, God uses the spinning motion to make us into His masterpiece. You and I are chosen vessels. I am reminded again of this Scripture promise: "For we are His workmanship, created in Christ Jesus for good works, which God prepared beforehand that we should walk in them" (Ephesians 2:10 NKJV).

The word translated here as *workmanship* or in other translations as *masterpiece* is the Greek word *poiema*, which is:

> A design produced by an artisan. *Poiema* emphasizes God as the Master Designer, the universe as His creation (Romans 1:20), and the redeemed believer as His new creation (Ephesians 2:10). Before conversion our lives had no rhyme or reason. Conversion brought us balance, symmetry, and order. We are God's poem, His work of art.[1]

At the time you are experiencing a traumatic event in your life, it doesn't feel like you have balance, symmetry, and order. Yet God, as the artisan, knows what is required for you and me to become who we are called to be. It does *not* mean that God purposefully plans for evil things to happen in our lives. What the Enemy means for evil in our lives, God works for good.

Jesus Overcame Death

In this life, death feels permanent. But Jesus overcame death, hell, and the grave when He was crucified, died, and rose again to life.

The first to witness Jesus' resurrection was Mary Magdalene. She was one of the women disciples who followed Jesus. There is no evidence from Scripture that Mary Magdalene was a prostitute. But Scripture does give an account of her being set free from demonic oppression:

> Jesus began a tour of the nearby towns and villages, preaching and announcing the Good News about the Kingdom of God. He took his twelve disciples with him, along with some women who had been cured of evil spirits and diseases. Among them were Mary Magdalene, from whom he had cast out seven demons.
>
> Luke 8:1–2

As a woman set free, Mary was a devoted disciple, who traveled with Jesus and the other disciples. The fact that these women were a part of the traveling team shows Jesus' respect for both men and women. He did not view women as property; He valued what they contributed in ministry.

Mary showed her loyalty to Jesus by staying with Him through His deepest pain. Along with Mary the mother of Jesus, she witnessed Jesus' torture and crucifixion. The traumatic loss of Jesus crushed all of her hopes for the future. She had given her life to follow and serve Jesus, and now He was gone. Nothing prepared her for what she would experience:

> Early in the morning on the first day of the week, while it was still dark, Mary Magdalene came to the tomb and saw that the stone was moved away from the entrance. She ran at once to Simon Peter and the other disciple, the one Jesus loved, breathlessly panting, "They took the Master from the tomb. We don't know where they've put him."
>
> John 20:1–2 MSG

Peter and John raced to the tomb. John outran Peter, but it was Peter who first looked inside and found pieces of linen cloth neatly folded. When John went into the tomb and saw the evidence, he believed that Jesus had risen from the dead.

Peter and John went back home, but Mary lingered:

> But Mary stood outside the tomb weeping. As she wept, she knelt
> to look into the tomb and saw two angels sitting there, dressed in
> white, one at the head, the other at the foot of where Jesus' body
> had been laid. They said to her, "Woman, why do you weep?"
>
> "They took my Master," she said, "and I don't know where
> they put him." After she said this, she turned away and saw Jesus
> standing there. But she didn't recognize him.
>
> Jesus spoke to her, "Woman, why do you weep? Who are you
> looking for?"
>
> She, thinking that he was the gardener, said, "Mister, if you took
> him, tell me where you put him so I can care for him."
>
> Jesus said, "Mary."
>
> Turning to face him, she said in Hebrew, "*Rabboni!*" meaning
> "Teacher!"
>
> Jesus said, "Don't cling to me, for I have not yet ascended to the
> Father. Go to my brothers and tell them, 'I ascend to my Father
> and your Father, my God and your God.'"
>
> Mary Magdalene went, telling the news to the disciples: "I saw
> the Master!" And she told them everything he said to her.
>
> vv. 11–18 MSG

Nothing prepared Mary for finding the tomb empty and then
having a conversation with Jesus himself. Jesus helped Mary to
see beyond the temporary boundaries of life on earth and pointed
her to the greater reality of eternity. Suddenly her pain and loss
were turned into triumph and victory. She was a firsthand witness
of the truth of the Resurrection.

The Promise of Life after Death

I was thirty-one years old and six months pregnant when I got the
call that my father was facing life-and-death surgery. Making ar-
rangements for my three children, I hurried to my father's side in
the hospital. After spending time with him in his room, I marched

to the hospital chapel, ready to fight in prayer. I had just taught on the power of God to heal. These promises of healing came to mind as I considered that my dad was only sixty-one with his sixty-second birthday around the corner. He had a lot of life to live. I needed him. My children needed him. He hadn't even met the baby in my womb.

There had been many other times that I had prayed and seen God heal. Many women facing infertility are now happy mothers of children after we prayed. I witnessed a deaf woman who was part of our life group have her hearing completely restored. I have witnessed God heal all types of diseases as a result of prayer. I was full of faith. Of course God would heal my dad.

As I knelt down and looked up at the chapel altar, God spoke to my heart. He very clearly said, *"I'm taking your father home."* I was shocked. Dad was too young to die. But I knew God's voice, and I felt His peace warm and comfort me.

A few days later, the doctors came back from surgery and gave us their findings. My dad's entire body was filled with cancer. His liver, his kidneys, his stomach, and his colon were cancer-ridden. Death was imminent.

As a family we sat together in the waiting room, shell-shocked and weeping from the news. Then my brother Dave, a skilled storyteller, began to fill the room with stories about Dad. Dad was a man of great influence, skill, and success, but he was also hilarious. God took our sorrow and turned it into joy as we began to celebrate his life.

Three weeks later, when I walked into the flower-filled church that held my father's body in the coffin, it was clear. Dad was not there. He was in heaven with Jesus. My overwhelming pain and loss were swallowed up by the comfort of heaven.

Heaven Is Real

With my father's death, the knowledge of heaven became very real to my heart. During the three weeks prior to his death, Dad had one foot on earth and one in heaven. He was a man who kept current on the news. Yet from the time he stepped foot into the hospital, he didn't read a newspaper or watch the news. At one point, when we thought he would die that night, we gathered around his bedside in prayer and sang hymns of praise, sensing heaven's gates ready to welcome him home.

Before Jesus died on the cross, He had talked to His disciples about what was going to happen. They didn't understand His words at the time. It was as John looked back that the Holy Spirit inspired him to record these words of Jesus:

> Let not your heart be troubled; you believe in God, believe also in Me. In My Father's house are many mansions; if it were not so, I would have told you. I go to prepare a place for you. And if I go and prepare a place for you, I will come again and receive you to Myself; that where I am, there you may be also.
>
> 14:1–3 NKJV

Jesus was preparing those He loved for His imminent death as well as their future hope: the wonder of the Father's house being prepared for those who believe. Jesus has prepared a way for us to live with Him eternally.

Being a believer in Jesus Christ makes our prayers at death different than if we didn't believe in an afterlife. Our hearts long for a future world. We may not realize it, but the life that we live on earth will never totally satisfy our hearts. Unfinished business, imperfection, failure, loneliness, pain, loss, and disappointment all vanish in heaven. Torment, trial, deception, rejection, and trauma do not pass through the gates of heaven.

Peace illuminates our hearts and minds when we realize we are citizens of another kingdom. Our sojourn here is temporal, filled with tests and trials that will pass away. But our prayer lives will continue into eternity. Our conversation with God will be unending and unhindered by all the confusion of life on this earth.

If you receive Jesus as your Lord and Savior in this life, you will eternally be in God's presence. He will wipe away all of your tears and fears. Every disappointment will be turned into the hope of eternity. The promise of heaven is real for those who believe.

Resurrection Overwhelms Pain and Loss

Jesus' resurrection takes the sting out of pain and loss. His resurrection changes everything! All of our lives are reframed by the truth of His victory over death. Jesus' resurrection is the firstfruits of eternal life for all who believe:

> But in fact, Christ has been raised from the dead. He is the first of a great harvest of all who have died. So you see, just as death came into the world through a man, now the resurrection from the dead has begun through another man. Just as everyone dies because we all belong to Adam, everyone who belongs to Christ will be given new life. But there is an order to this resurrection: Christ was raised as the first of the harvest; then all who belong to Christ will be raised when he comes back. . . . Then, when our dying bodies have been transformed into bodies that will never die, this Scripture will be fulfilled: "Death is swallowed up in victory. O death, where is your victory? O death, where is your sting?"
>
> 1 Corinthians 15:20–23, 54–55

When sin first came into the world through Adam and Eve, our world went spinning out of control. Prior to the fall of humanity, our world was perfect. There was no disease, death, or even weeds to pull in the garden. There were no hurricanes, earthquakes, tornados, or tsunamis. We would have been free even from the bacteria that cause bad breath and decay.

It's hard to imagine this perfect world, yet we long for it from the depths of who we are. We know when things are not right and we feel powerless to change what is beyond our control. Yet this itself is our victory. We can cast every sin, weight, trauma, and loss onto Jesus, who overcame. We can't stop the world from spinning, but the One who put it in motion in the first place will hold our world together even when it seems to be falling apart.

Replacing Pain and Loss with Hope

The hope we have is anchored in the redeeming love of our Savior. Pain and loss will change our perspective, but we can choose how it changes us. We can become *bitter* or *better*. The choice is ours.

Pain that is deep and cuts into our soul is often beyond words. It's so like God to provide a way for us to pray that is beyond the words that we can speak:

> And the Holy Spirit helps us in our weakness. For example, we don't know what God wants us to pray for. But the Holy Spirit prays for us with groanings that cannot be expressed in words. And the Father who knows all hearts knows what the Spirit is saying, for the Spirit pleads for us believers in harmony with God's own will.
>
> Romans 8:26–27

At times of my deepest pain and loss, my prayer often begins with lying facedown, groaning and weeping before God. Because I trust Him, I don't have to hold it all together. In my weakness, I know He will be strong. I can completely fall apart, knowing that He is the One who takes the spinning of my world and like a potter uses it to make me into the masterpiece that He always knew I would be.

Reading the Bible and praying calibrates your brain cells. Every day you are bombarded by the depressing echo of the world. You can replace the traumatic pain and loss that you have suffered in the past with the present and future hope of Jesus Christ.

Hope is confident expectation in God. God is the fulfillment of all of your hopes and dreams. Hope rises from the ashes of destruction. Hope overpowers sarcasm and cynicism. Hope is eternal. Hope is a settled certainty in God's answered prayers. Christian hope is more than a wish or a desire. Hope is the light of God that overwhelms darkness.

A helpful acronym for hope is:

> H—Hold
> O—on
> P—Pain
> E—Ends

We most need to hang on to hope when everything in our life is pointing to death and destruction. Depression begins when hope ends. The difference between those of us who throw in the towel and quit and those who rebuild and keep going is summarized in one word—*hope*.

Replacing pain and loss with God's hope is built on our joy-filled anticipation of God making all things right. Pain and loss come in all shapes and sizes in our lives. It may be losing a loved one, a job, or friends. The pain of loss we feel through betrayal, rejection, and abandonment can hang on us like graveclothes unless we cast off the death they bring to our emotions and replace it with the hope of Jesus.

It's important for you to realize in prayer that you can't fix everything. There are situations in your life that you won't have the full perspective on until you are with Jesus. You and I will look back at the petty things that brought us pain and see the wind of His Spirit blow it away.

Setbacks in your life are often setups for Jesus to use you. Let's allow the Potter to use the pain in our lives to make us vessels of honor. You can try to fight against the Potter's hand and how He is shaping you, or you can embrace the process of transformation. Being on the Potter's wheel will take time. In fact, it will take your whole life and into eternity.

~PRAY~

God, you are the Potter, I am the clay. When my life is spinning out of control, I choose to believe that my life is in your hands and that you are bringing purpose out of my pain.

Creative Artisan, my life has been marred by destruction and loss. Take the ugly things that the Enemy meant for evil and make me a masterpiece in your hands. I trust you to shape me.

I know that I can't go backward. I can only go forward.

Jesus, thank you for being the same yesterday, today, and forever. You are my future and my hope. I anticipate being in your presence for all of eternity. I choose you as my Lord and Savior. I turn away from the sin and destruction of my past. I surrender to your perfecting will in my life. I forgive those who have used and abused me. I turn them over to your care. They are also on your Potter's wheel. I trust you to change them as you are also changing me. And I entrust to your care those whom I have loved and lost.

You are the resurrection and the life. With joy-filled anticipation, I look forward to the day of being in heaven with you and all those who love your name. Holy Spirit, I thank you that you are the down payment and the guarantee of eternity.

Fill me afresh with your Spirit. Comfort me in my loss. Empower me to make a difference here on earth. Make my life count. You are my joy and delight. I trust you. In Jesus' name I pray, amen.

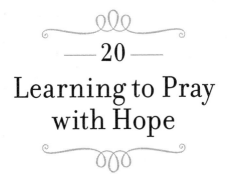

— 20 —

Learning to Pray with Hope

If you base your hope in the material world, you are bound to be disappointed. Abraham is the father of our faith. It took over two decades for God's promises to Abraham to be fulfilled. When you have a promise that takes a long time to be fulfilled, it can cause you to be discouraged. Hope is an anchor for our souls.

1. Read Romans 5:1–5. How does God overcome disappointment?
2. Read Romans 8:1. What is the difference between condemnation and conviction?
3. Read Romans 8:2–4. What do you learn from this passage of Scripture?
4. Read Romans 8:5–9. What is God saying to you in these verses?
5. Read Romans 8:10–11. What is significant in these two verses?
6. Read Romans 8:12–17. What two things do you share with Christ?
7. Read Romans 8:18–25. What is all of creation waiting for?
8. Read Romans 8:26–27. How does the Holy Spirit help us?

9. Read Romans 8:28. Write down this verse and memorize it. What two things are required for the promise of Romans 8:28 to be fulfilled?

10. Read Romans 8:29–30. What did God do for you?

11. Read Romans 8:31–39 in several different translations. What can separate you from God's love? How is God speaking to you through these verses?

12. Read Romans 12:12. What do you learn about prayer in this passage?

13. Read Romans 15:13. Who is the source of our hope?

14. Read 1 Corinthians 13:4–7. What do you learn here about hope?

15. Read Ephesians 1:18. What is the hope God gives to those He has called?

16. Read Hebrews 10:23. What do you hold tightly?

17. Read Hebrews 11:1. How do faith and hope relate?

Overcoming Emotional Pain and Loss

When you experience a painful loss, you may go through stages of grief. Elisabeth Kübler-Ross introduced five stages of grief[1] that many experience. Stage 1 is *denial*: You feel like this can't be happening. Stage 2 is *anger*: You realize your powerlessness to change the situation and sometimes look for someone to blame. Stage 3 is *bargaining*: You try to see if there is anything you can do to change the situation. Stage 4 is *depression*: Your emotions are turned inward and you feel like giving up. Stage 5 *acceptance*: You know you can't change what has happened, but you begin to move forward with the next phase of your life. You may not experience grief in the order of these stages, but it will take time to go through the process of healing in your life.

18. Read Job 1:1–22. What do you learn from this passage about how to face trauma? Focus on Job's initial response to his loss in Job 1:20–22. What do you learn in these verses?

19. If you are in the middle of a painful situation right now, consider reading through the entire book of Job in one sitting. Notice how little his friends are able to help Job deal with his pain and loss. Read Job 38. What do you learn from Job's encounter with God? Read Job 42:7–16. How does Job's story conclude?

20. Take out your journal or download pages from www.Sue Detweiler.com and begin writing about one of the most difficult life experiences you have faced. After you have written out your story, listen to what God may be saying to you. Skip a line and write down His words and Scriptures that come to your mind as you listen for His voice.

Praying with Boldness, Confidence, and Grace

Our confidence goes beyond what we experience here on earth. Our hope is anchored in an eternal reality. Jesus is God in human flesh. He understands the depth of your pain, loss, rejection, and betrayal. He went through all of what we go through in life—every human emotion that you can or will experience—and yet He did not sin.

We are able to pray with boldness, confidence, and grace when we encounter Jesus and receive the hope that He brings.

21. Read Matthew 26:39. How did Jesus pray when He faced the cross? How does this impact your prayers when you face something difficult?

22. Read Hebrews 6:18–19. How does hope anchor your soul?

23. Read 1 Corinthians 15. How does the power of the Resurrection give you hope?

Replacing Pain and Loss with Hope

Pain and loss look to the past.

Trauma marks us.

We can't escape pain and loss in this life.

The Lies of Pain and Loss

You will never get better.

You will never be able to get back on track.

You will never fulfill your destiny.

The Truth of Hope

God's hope is anchored in a higher reality.

God's healing transforms our lives.

God's hope of salvation never disappoints.

We can be confident in eternal hope.

Extending God's Grace

In order to fulfill God's call on your life, there is a spiritual struggle you go through in prayer. Through overcoming our hardships, we can reach out to others and offer hope.

For Group Discussion

Bonus Video: I share a time when I overcame loss with hope. Watch this bonus video at www.SueDetweiler.com.

24. When was the last time you lost hope? Were you praying? Or avoiding God and spending time in your loss rather than in prayer and praise?

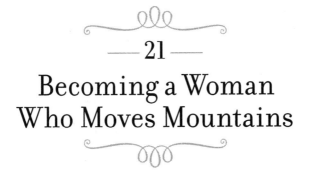

— 21 —

Becoming a Woman
Who Moves Mountains

Wow! We have traveled so far together. Yes, we have battle wounds just like warriors do. We have overcome so much! The good news is that through the battles we become more like Jesus. Just pause a moment and reflect with joy that the battle belongs to the Lord! Because of what Jesus did on the cross, you are able to confidently say:

I believe.
I am chosen.
I am healed.
I am honored.
I am secure.
I am transformed.
I am empowered.
I am humble.
I am bold.
I am expectant.

God is so amazing! He loves you and sacrificed His life so you could be transformed daily. You are transforming

fear into faith
rejection into calling
brokenness into wholeness
shame into grace
anxiety into peace
sadness into joy
perfectionism into presence
entitlement into humility
timidity into boldness
disappointment and loss into hope

Even when it seems like nothing is happening in your life, you are being transformed. Your character is becoming more like Christ. The fuel of this transformation is your prayers and the prayers of those who love you. You may not feel like a woman who moves mountains, but that is who you have become and are becoming as you walk by faith and not by sight (2 Corinthians 5:7 NKJV). Your prayers are changing lives. The first life that is being changed is yours!

Yes, it may be a long road ahead that will require each of us to walk in endurance. *But, girl, you are confident, bold, and full of God's grace.* With incredible gratitude you are able to say in faith that "if God is for me, who can be against me?" (see Romans 8:31). And I want to say to you:

God is for you!
He's got your back!
Whatever you are facing, He's bigger!
You are no longer a victim, you are a victor!
Now be strong and courageous!

Don't forget your destiny!
He has plans and a purpose for you!
He will turn your past junk into great gain!
Don't give up!

So many times our breakthrough in God is a short distance ahead. The Enemy wants to get us to stop short of God's fullness for our lives. Remember who you are, and who God has called you to be.

The prophet Jeremiah laments the fall of Jerusalem. In his lament, he gives a reason for her fall. She forgot her destiny: "Her uncleanness is in her skirts; *she did not consider her destiny;* therefore her collapse was awesome" (Lamentations 1:9 NKJV).

She forgot her destiny, fell into immorality, and collapsed. That's what happens to each of us when we forget who we are called to be. You and I need to remember God's plan and purpose for our lives. Make it a part of your daily prayer life to highlight and write down specific verses from Scripture that captivate you. Meditate on those Scriptures and turn them into Scripture prayers. Read and rehearse His Word as a part of your prayers. Remember your destiny in Him. When you open your prayer journal, expect God to speak specifically to you about your present situation. As you hear God's voice speaking, write down the words you hear Him saying. Recording these words will help you remember specifically what you felt like God was saying as you encountered Him in prayer.

So as we conclude, let's remember who we are in Christ. Remember all the promises God has given you personally from the time you became a Christian until now. Remember, you are God's masterpiece; He created you anew in Christ Jesus, so you can do the good things He planned for you long ago (see Ephesians 2:10).

You go, girl! God's got this! You are much stronger and farther along than you feel you are! You are not who you used to be. You are a new creation in Christ. You have a destiny!

PART TWO

Introduction

I prepared a gift for you! Yes, a gift. Maybe you are like me. I tend to drift away from fully believing who I am in Christ. Somehow, unbelief comes into my mindset. I get discouraged and battle worn and I need to find a way to calibrate my soul. Sometimes it's the sin that is hidden from me that I need to confess. I may be hurt by someone, and I need to choose to forgive them. Other times, it's just the uncleanness of the world we live in. Stuff happens all the time. If you travel, you may turn on the TV in the hotel room, and all of a sudden you are viewing pornographic pictures that you didn't expect to see. You didn't commit a sin, yet the unclean pictures plague your mind. This is an example of what life can be like. We live in an unclean and fallen world. But Jesus is the bridegroom, and we are His bride. He gave himself for His bride "that He might sanctify and cleanse her with the washing of water by the word" (Ephesians 5:26 NKJV).

You and I are cleansed by God's Word. We need His Word to wash our minds of the unclean things in the world. These things become like a weight to us and they drag down our joy-filled love life with God.

Part two of this book is meant to be a resource guide that you can come back to and use to calibrate your heart and mind with the power of the Word. Included in this guide are

21 Days to Spiritual Breakthrough to provide a springboard to spending time with God

Guidelines for Taking a Spiritual Retreat to get away to reflect and listen to God

Guidelines for Fasting to focus your prayers

5 Steps of Grace to help bring healing and deliverance to your life (Download at www.SueDetweiler.com)

I commend you on your journey to becoming a woman who moves mountains. Know that I am cheering for you along with others who have gone before you in your spiritual journey. Be encouraged by this word:

> Therefore we also, since we are surrounded by so great a cloud of witnesses, let us lay aside every weight, and the sin which so easily ensnares us, and let us run with endurance the race that is set before us, looking unto Jesus, the author and finisher of our faith, who for the joy that was set before Him endured the cross, despising the shame, and has sat down at the right hand of the throne of God.
>
> Hebrews 12:1–2 NKJV

Truly, there is a cloud of witnesses cheering you on. Just like the women who shared their testimonies in *Women Who Move Mountains,* as you lay aside the *weight* and the *sin* and run your race with *endurance*, you are going to cross the finish line. *You can do it!* Just keep looking toward Jesus and away from rejection, fear, shame, and all the difficult things you have experienced. *You are a woman who moves mountains! Your life has been transformed and is being transformed. You can walk in fresh confidence, boldness, and grace!*

5 Steps of Grace is an ebook that will provide a thorough cleansing from sin and bring God's deliverance. You can download it at www.SueDetweiler.com. This resource guide may be something that you will want to use at the beginning of every new year.

21 Days to Spiritual Breakthrough

Introduction

Let's take the next twenty-one days to refocus, recharge, and restore the vital energy of who God has made us to be. The devotional guide has a simple format that is meant to be interactive. Each day includes the following elements:

journal Use this question as a springboard to apply the devotional to your life by journaling your response. Go deeper than a yes or no answer.

meditate Your life will change as you meditate on God's Word. Choose your favorite version of the Scripture and spend time committing it to memory.

devotional These words are to help you become devoted to Christ.

pray aloud Read these prayers out loud.

declare Speak this declaration and let it become fuel for prayer. Joel 3:10 (NKJV) says, "Let the weak say, 'I am strong.'"

In the midst of spiritual warfare, it is helpful to speak out of your mouth the truth of who you are because of what Jesus did for you on the cross.

Together we stand at a threshold of gaining greater clarity and focus for our lives. Another resource for you is daily audio encouragement. If you would like to receive the one-minute *Healing Rain Radio Feature* in your inbox on Monday through Friday, sign up at www.SueDetweiler.com.

Take a Spiritual Retreat

Look at your calendar and set aside at least one day for a spiritual retreat. This is a time to fast, pray, and seek God with your whole heart. *Guidelines for Taking a Spiritual Retreat* are included at the end of *21 Days to Spiritual Breakthrough*.

Day 1

Hunger

What types of things do you crave? Is there a particular appetite in your life that conflicts with your love for God?

meditate

You're blessed when you've worked up a good appetite for God. He's food and drink in the best meal you'll ever eat.

Matthew 5:6 MSG

devotional

Our appetites reveal a lot about who we are. God has made us to crave. He has put within us desires that can only be satisfied by Him.

Too often in my life I have found myself turning to food when I really need God's comfort. I find myself standing by the pantry wanting to fill up my need. Or turning on Netflix to escape from my life. Do you have things that you turn to rather than God when you feel anxious, afraid, or even bored?

The deceptive sugar of this world will never satisfy or fulfill our spiritual appetites. Like cotton candy, it may taste good for a moment, but it quickly melts in your mouth, leaving a residue that causes spiritual decay. We need to develop a healthy appetite for God. He's the One who will satisfy your deepest hunger. You will hunger for what you have been feeding on. Feast on God.

pray aloud

Loving God, awaken my senses to desire you. I have feasted on the world's fare. Like cotton candy, it tasted sweet at first, but it had no substance. Help me to hunger for the meat of your Word. Teach me to desire time with you. Help me to turn away from a worldly appetite and develop a healthy hunger for you. In Jesus' name, amen.

declare

I am hungry for God.

Day 2

Thirst

journal

Does your life sometimes feel boring or dry? What do you long for?

meditate

A white-tailed deer drinks from the creek;
I want to drink God, deep draughts of God.
I'm thirsty for God-alive.
I wonder, "Will I ever make it—arrive and drink in God's
   presence?"
I'm on a diet of tears—tears for breakfast, tears for supper.
All day long people knock at my door,
Pestering, "Where is this God of yours?"

Psalm 42:1–3 MSG

devotional

If you hunger and thirst for God's righteousness, you will be filled
(Matthew 5:6 NKJV). Thirst is not just the dryness you feel in your

mouth when you need water; it is the longing in your heart for more of God. Do you crave God like the deer pants for water in a brook? Do you come to God with your own brokenness and need that can only be met in His presence?

A drought in your soul often forms from a misplaced passion. If you turn to the world, it's like drinking from a dirty vessel. If you drink from it long enough, you will get used to it. But when you drink from the cool, clean, purifying presence of God, you will thirst for more of Him.

pray aloud

I thirst for you, God. My life is dry without the stream of your presence. Quench the deep desire of my heart as I drink deeply from your Word. In your name I pray, amen.

declare

I am thirsty for God.

Day 3
Hope

Do you find yourself struggling with disappointment? What helps you overcome this?

Hope will not lead to disappointment. For we know how dearly God loves us, because he has given us the Holy Spirit to fill our hearts with his love.

Romans 5:5

Disappointment grows when the soil of our heart is hopeless. You may feel like a task is impossible to accomplish or that you are inadequate to fulfill your purpose. Setbacks can become setups when we cleanse our minds of negative thoughts.

Hope arises from the dust of disappointment. It frames its optimism on the truth of God's eternal love. The Holy Spirit guides our thinking to be filled with expectation. God will meet us where we are. He will both comfort and challenge us.

Let confident expectation guide you through the threshold of your new beginning. Put your faith in the person of Jesus Christ. His promises will never fail.

pray aloud

God of comfort and understanding, you know the frailty of my life. You know the negative cycles of my thoughts. Cleanse my mind with your perspective. Fill my heart with your hope.

As I surrender my life to you, fill me afresh with your hope. In Jesus' name, amen.

declare

I am filled with hope.

Day 4

Patience

Do you find yourself struggling with patience? Write down an example of where you are presently struggling with impatience in your life.

meditate

> There's more to come: We continue to shout our praise even when we're hemmed in with troubles, because we know how troubles can develop passionate patience in us, and how that patience in turn forges the tempered steel of virtue, keeping us alert for whatever God will do next. In alert expectancy such as this, we're never left feeling shortchanged. Quite the contrary—we can't round up enough containers to hold everything God generously pours into our lives through the Holy Spirit!
>
> Romans 5:3–5 MSG

devotional

Did you know that when you face obstacles in your life, you have an opportunity to develop passionate patience? Troubles can be turned into tempered steel of virtue in your character. Difficulties can cause you to stay alert with expectancy for what God is up to.

God is so generous toward you in thought, word, and deed that you couldn't round up enough containers to hold everything He wants to pour into your life.

So the next time you are feeling impatience run through your veins, change the atmosphere of your soul by trusting that God's got it.

pray aloud

Thank you for building patience into my character. You are the Master-Builder, God. You have a design of who you are making me to be. Let the sandpaper of difficult situations smooth out the rough and jagged edges of my thinking. You are a patient God. Make my character reflect your long-suffering. I love you with all of my heart. In Jesus' name, amen.

declare

I am patient.

Day 5

Greatness

journal

Is it difficult to see yourself as someone who was born to be great?

meditate

> Christ in you, the hope of glory.
>
> Colossians 1:27 NKJV

devotional

You have been born to be great. God wove you together while you were in your mother's womb. The essence of your greatness is that Christ is in you. It's His life in you that gives you hope of glory.

God's greatness is revealed in you when you live your life like Christ did. He didn't consider himself above everyone else. He humbled himself, put on the apron of a hired hand, and served people. He tirelessly made himself available to care for others.

Greatness is walking in humility before God. Our confidence comes through surrender. Greatness does not mean that we are entitled to things or deserve better. You are not called to be a narcissist who thinks you are better than everyone else. Greatness in God's kingdom means that you are a servant of all. If you understand the greatness that God calls you to, you will know that it's not about you. It's a call to lay down your life for others.

Are you taking the time to lay down your life for others? Are you putting their needs before your own? Are you serving God with your whole heart?

No matter where you are in your walk with God, you can begin now. Your hope of glory is allowing Christ in you to shine outward, His love coming through you to others.

pray aloud

Amazing God, your gentleness has made me great. You are my hope and expectation. Help me to walk in the fullness of my calling. I humble myself before you and surrender my will. I know that true greatness is born on the shoulders of humility. I embrace your meekness. I choose to serve you and others for your glory. In Jesus' name, amen.

declare

I am great by God's grace.

Day 6

Repentance

journal

Describe a time when you felt the conviction of the Holy Spirit.

meditate

If we confess our sins, He is faithful and just to forgive us our sins
and to cleanse us from all unrighteousness.

1 John 1:9 NKJV

devotional

In the beauty of the spring, I will spend many hours on my knees on
my garden, planting with the hope of a beautiful array of flowers.
In the summer, I will often be on my knees pulling weeds in the
same garden. God spoke to me about sin through a particularly
hardy weed in Tennessee that I combatted week after week. I would
dig down and pull out that weed only for it to pop up a few feet
away. It had such an underground hold in that particular garden
that it seemed impossible to pull up and root out.

Sin often has an underground root system similar to weeds. Repentance requires you and me to go deep down to the hidden motivations of our hearts. Repentance is changing your mind and perspective. It's God's goodness that leads you to repentance. The Holy Spirit reveals what's hidden from sight.

Sin comes out of our heart through the confession of our mouth. Confession means that we are agreeing with God. Repentance provides a powerful opportunity for a changed life. Genuine repentance is a change of heart toward God and others and will lead to a new way of thinking about life.

Today, allow the Holy Spirit to search your heart. Acknowledge each wrong thought, word, action, or attitude in order for true transformation to take place. The Holy Spirit will cleanse and refine you from the inside out.

pray aloud

Merciful God, shine your light into the recesses of my thoughts and motives of my heart.

It's your goodness, Lord, that leads me to repentance. Alert me to those sins and habits that keep coming back like weeds. I choose to tend to the garden of my life. Let your refreshing rains soften the soil of my heart. I love you. Amen.

declare

By God's grace, I am pure.

Day 7

Persevering

Describe a situation that makes you want to give up. How has God helped you to be persistent?

meditate

> You need to persevere so that when you have done the will of God, you will receive what he has promised.
>
> Hebrews 10:36 NIV

devotional

Perseverance in prayer is a powerful tool in the hand of God. Prayer doesn't change God, it changes you and me. To be long-suffering is to be like God who persists with each one of us.

When my daughter Hannah was in fifth grade, all the children in her Sunday school class took their moms out for a Mother's Day tea. They made cards for us and then each daughter shared a word that described her mom. Hannah chose *persevering* for me. I was surprised by her thoughtful response and the use of this big word for a fifth grader.

As we were driving home, I thanked Hannah and asked her why she chose that word. She said, "You remember when you were painting our bedroom ceiling? Even though your neck was hurting as you leaned back and looked at the ceiling, you kept going and you didn't quit."

Sometimes in life we need to just keep going and not quit. We must put one foot in front of the other as we obey God in our daily lives.

pray aloud

Loving God, thank you that you don't give up on me. Thank you for filling me with your persevering love. Help me to persevere and do your will. I believe you for your promises to be fulfilled in my life. Awaken within me the desire, focus, and determination to keep going. In your strength and power, I pray, amen.

declare

I am persevering.

Day 8

Love

journal

Describe what makes you feel loved. In his book *The Five Love Languages*, Gary Chapman describes five ways of sharing love. Which helps you to experience love the most: time, touch, affirmative words, gifts, or acts of service?

meditate

> What marvelous love the Father has extended to us! Just look at it—we're called children of God! That's who we really are. But that's also why the world doesn't recognize us or take us seriously, because it has no idea who he is or what he's up to.
>
> 1 John 3:1 MSG

devotional

God's love for us is unconditional and unending. He loves like a father loves his children. His intense affection toward us is not based on our actions or our attitudes. It's impossible to truly comprehend unconditional love. The closest example we have is a love of a father or a mother for their child.

God's love is generous. "For God so loved the world that He gave His only begotten Son, that whoever believes in Him should not perish but have everlasting life" (John 3:16 NKJV). It's impossible to outgive God.

God's love is creative. As the Creator of all things, His very nature is to love. He created us to be in relationship with Him and with others. We are admonished to love others: "Beloved, let us love one another, for love is of God; and everyone who loves is born of God and knows God. He who does not love does not know God, for God is love" (1 John 4:7–8 NKJV).

God's love is eternal. His love never ends. He never gives up on you. He never quits. He won't abandon you. He promises that He "will never leave you nor forsake you" (Hebrews 13:5 NKJV). Today, know that you are loved.

pray aloud

You are love, God. Your love never ends. Your love reaches to the heavens. Your love reaches to the earth. Your love mends hearts. Your love awakens souls. Your love surrounds me. Your love will never fail. I love you. Amen.

declare

I am loved.

Day 9

Faith

Do you like rewards? Are you willing to put your faith into action?

meditate

> But without faith it is impossible to please Him, for he who comes to God must believe that He is, and that He is a rewarder of those who diligently seek Him.
>
> Hebrews 11:6 NKJV

devotional

You and I please God and show that we love Him when we obey His commandments.

If you are a part-time believer who tends to check out when the going gets tough, you won't gain the fullness of what God has for you. If you want an immediate and eternal reward, walk in faith. When you diligently seek God, it's guaranteed that your life will turn around.

Faith is having complete trust and confidence in God. Faith is action. It is more than a mental assent; it is a willingness to move forward without compromise. Faith means that you are going to rely completely on God. Because we trust God, faith is being committed to do the right thing.

Faith finds security in God alone. You are loyal to His call in your life. Love and obedience follow true faith. Faith is anchored on the truth of who God is. Results of faith are seen in the radical changes in your life as you walk out your faith daily.

pray aloud

Almighty God, I anchor my faith in you. I choose to diligently seek you. I am turning away from my old attachments and turning to you in faith. God, I am confident that you will not only provide for me but also launch me into my destiny. Help me to be faithful to follow your call completely. I love you. Amen.

declare

I am full of faith.

Day 10

Diligence

Describe a time when you became more serious about your relationship with God. How do you become more diligent in seeking to follow God?

meditate

> Keep your heart with all diligence, for out of it spring the issues of life.
>
> Proverbs 4:23 NKJV

> We want each of you to show this same diligence to the very end, so that what you hope for may be fully realized. We do not want you to become lazy, but to imitate those who through faith and patience inherit what has been promised.
>
> Hebrews 6:11–12 NIV

devotional

Diligence is careful and persistent work with effort. To be diligent is to work hard to attain a goal. Diligence is to be thorough, complete, and persistent in your actions.

To keep your heart with diligence means that you are responsible for what you allow into your heart and what you keep out. By listening to the Holy Spirit, you are the reliable gatekeeper of your heart. No one else is able to guard the wellspring of life. You are the one who will stand before God and give an account of how you stewarded your life. The key is to be diligent to guard your heart from evil and give your heart to good.

pray aloud

Holy Spirit, put a gate on my heart. Help me to discern between good and evil. Help me to study the Word of God to know what is truly good and noble. I choose to nurture the wellspring of my life, which is my connection with you. Let the purity of your stream of holiness flow from me to others. It's in Jesus' name I pray, amen.

declare

I am diligent.

Day 11

Suffering

journal

Describe a time of suffering in your life. How do you deal with your emotions as you go through suffering? Do you stuff your emotions? Do you deny your emotions? Do you medicate your emotions with drugs, alcohol, or food?

meditate

I want to know Christ—yes, to know the power of his resurrection and participation in his sufferings, becoming like him in his death, and so, somehow, attaining to the resurrection from the dead.

Philippians 3:10–11 NIV

devotional

Have you gone through a period of suffering in your life and then gotten to the other side of it and found that you are a better person because of the suffering? That has been true for my life. When I go through suffering, I am marked by compassion and equipped to help others go through suffering toward maturity in Christ.

Part of how we get to know Jesus is to fellowship with Him in suffering. He's the one who suffered and died on the cross for us. But after His suffering, He rose from the dead and gave us eternal life.

Don't be discouraged. There's hope in the darkest and lowest places because you are not alone. Jesus is there. As you fellowship with Him in suffering, you will also be raised to walk in newness of life. There's hope shining light into the darkest night.

pray aloud

Jesus, everything that I do on my own is garbage compared to knowing you. I want to know you intimately and personally. I want to share in your suffering and pain, rejoicing with you in resurrection, being raised to walk in newness of life. I trust you to heal me and make me more like you. Amen.

declare

I am raised with Christ.

Day 12

Forgiveness

journal

What is more difficult for you—to forgive yourself for mistakes or to forgive others who have hurt you?

meditate

> Make a clean break with all cutting, backbiting, profane talk. Be gentle with one another, sensitive. Forgive one another as quickly and thoroughly as God in Christ forgave you.
>
> Ephesians 4:31–32 MSG

devotional

It may be difficult for each of us to forgive because we need to have a better understanding of what forgiveness is and what it is not. Forgiveness is giving the situation over to God and trusting in Him to bring justice. Forgiveness is not letting the offender continue to hurt, wound, or abuse you. It is important to hold others accountable for their actions. Forgiveness is not continuing to be a victim. Forgiveness is making a choice to forgive. Forgiveness is a process, not an event. Forgiveness is not forgetting, but it is moving forward into health.

Forgiveness should be a major part of our daily lives. It is a promise of freedom from the junk of the past and the freedom from toxic relationships and cultures. Forgiveness helps you to access the grace and mercy of God for yourself. You are forgiven by God as you forgive others.

pray aloud

Jesus, I embrace a lifestyle of daily forgiveness of others and of myself. You have modeled forgiveness. While you were yet on the cross you forgave the thief beside you. I choose to foster a heart that is ready to forgive on a daily basis. I choose to let go of grudges and trust you for justice. You are a good God. You are fair to me. Thank you for the freedom from offense and the cleansing of every hurt-filled attitude. I trust you. Amen.

declare

I am forgiven.

Day 13

Free

journal

Describe an area in your life where you desire to have more freedom.

meditate

For when we died with Christ we were set free from the power of sin.

Romans 6:7

devotional

Our freedom from sin is found as we daily die to our selfish desires. As we flee from the lust of our flesh, we gain a purity of heart, mind, and soul. The Enemy will make it seem like you lose your freedom when you surrender your whole heart to God. The truth is that through surrender you are truly free to be who God has made you to be.

Jesus died for our sin so that we can live free every day. His wounds heal us from the suffering and addictions of the world.

His death leads to your death. When you bring your temptation to God daily in prayer, He delivers and sets you free from bondage. You have greater confidence as you experience His transformation. Your growth in God is not a result of your own willpower, but a result of what Jesus has done through His death and resurrection.

pray aloud

Jesus, how can I thank you for what you have done on the cross for me? When you cried out, "It is finished," you freed me for all eternity. Now I pick up my cross and daily follow you. Free from sin's death and destruction. Free to live with hope and confidence. I celebrate you! Amen.

declare

I am free.

Day 14

~~~~~~

Courage

journal

Describe a time in your life when you felt like you were standing at
the edge of a precipice. What are you presently facing that requires
you to walk in courage?

meditate

> Have I not commanded you? Be strong and courageous. Do not be
> afraid; do not be discouraged, for the Lord your God will be with
> you wherever you go.
>
> Joshua 1:9 NIV

devotional

Read Joshua 1 and Romans 12:1–2.

After forty years of wandering around the desert eating manna
every day, Joshua was commissioned by God to take the Israelites
into the promised land. His leader and mentor, Moses, had died

in the wilderness and Joshua probably felt alone and afraid. The people had followed Moses. Would they follow him?

God got Joshua's attention by commanding him repeatedly to "be strong and courageous." He also promised Joshua that he was not alone. God was with him. In faith, Joshua had to let go of his grief and fear in order to rise up to his calling. God put His favor on Joshua and raised him up in the eyes of the Israelites. He had been faithfully serving beside Moses all of these years, but the people needed to see him in a new way and follow his leadership.

Joshua challenged the people to consecrate themselves and get ready to enter into the promised land. To consecrate means that we surrender our lives fully to God. We present ourselves as a living sacrifice (Romans 12:1). As we set our lives apart to serve God fully, we gain fresh courage to go where we have never gone before.

pray aloud

Powerful God, thank you for commanding me to be strong and courageous. I sometimes am tempted to hesitate and draw back. You charge me to not be afraid or discouraged. You call me to move forward in faith and courage. Thank you for your promise that you will be with me wherever I go. Take me into the promised land. I pray in your name, Jesus, amen.

declare

I am courageous.

Day 15

Boldness

Do you find yourself hesitating or drawing back when you should be moving forward in faith and boldness? Journal about a specific area where you need boldness in your life.

meditate

> Let us therefore come boldly to the throne of grace, that we may obtain mercy and find grace to help in time of need.
>
> Hebrews 4:16 NKJV

devotional

Read Hebrews 4:1–16.

One of my favorite scenes of the 1999 movie *Anna and the King* is when the little girl comes in to fetch her father, the king. Everyone in the room is bowing their heads to the ground out of reverence for the king, and Princess Fa-Ying pushes open the heavy doors and marches boldly to her father and crawls confidently into his arms and whispers in his ear. Even though the king is talking to dignitaries, he immediately responds to his daughter's request and carries her to the schoolroom to attend to her needs.

How much more boldly can we come to God's throne to obtain mercy and grace to help us in *our* time of need. We can crawl into daddy God's arms and know that He not only cares about our needs, but He is the most powerful One in the universe and makes things work for our good.

pray aloud

Father God, I boldly come to your throne, believing that you not only care for me and my needs, but that you will help me. I need your mercy and your grace to empower me. Help me to embrace you as my daddy and crawl into your lap without fear. You are the God of the universe. You are all-powerful. You are all-loving. I worship you, trust you, and love you with all of my heart. In the name of your Son I pray, amen.

declare

I am bold.

Day 16

Energy

journal

Do you feel like you are running out of steam at the end of the day? What wears you out? What energizes you?

meditate

Be energetic in your life of salvation, reverent and sensitive before God. That energy is God's energy, an energy deep within you, God himself willing and working at what will give him the most pleasure.

Philippians 2:13 MSG

devotional

Read Philippians 2:12–18.

Have you ever noticed that complaining and arguing zaps your strength, energy, and creativity? When you obey God, you will find Him at work in your life, giving you the desire and the power to do what pleases Him. When you live a life that is clean and pure on the inside, you will shine more brightly on the outside.

As you run your race of life, you will not run it in vain. Your life matters. Even if it feels like you are pouring out your life as a liquid offering to God, He will fill you up again with His joy. Today, find strength, encouragement, and energy from His Word. Remember, His hand is on your back as He whispers in your ear, "You can do it!"

pray aloud

God, you are the source of my life and strength. Empower me to run the race of faith with grace, energy, and insight. Help me know that I am not alone. Invigorate me with your love. Ignite my passion to follow you. Increase my focus so I may finish well. I trust you, Lord. In Jesus' name, amen.

declare

I am energetic.

Day 17

Purpose

journal

What is God's purpose for your life? As you write out a purpose statement, use Scriptures to remind you of your calling.

meditate

> For we are God's masterpiece. He has created us anew in Christ Jesus, so we can do the good things he planned for us long ago.
>
> Ephesians 2:10

devotional

Read Ephesians 2:1–10.

God is a master-designer, and you are His masterpiece. He gave you the blueprint for your life when He gave you the Bible. He has commissioned the Holy Spirit to be your contractor. He is constantly preparing you for the future.

All you need to do is trust God enough for Him to work in you and through you. He will use both your mistakes and your successes for His glory. It's God's redemptive gift from the beginning to the end. He wants you to join Him in the work that He is doing. Your salvation is a gift from Him. It's His kindness being poured out in your life. God prepared beforehand a path for you that you should walk in it. Be purposeful about the good things that He planned for you long ago.

pray aloud

Master-Designer, Creator God, wow! I'm amazed at the world you created for me to enjoy! The beauty of your creation is astounding. Yet you call me the masterpiece of your creation. How wonderful to have a plan and a purpose for my life that you prepared. Thank you for designing me with the gifts and talents uniquely fitting to my call. I commit to follow you and do the good things that you planned for me long ago. I love you, Jesus. In your name I pray, amen.

declare

I am a masterpiece.

Day 18

Tenacity

journal

To be tenacious is to hold fast and persist. Describe something in your life that you are tenacious about.

meditate

> My response is to get down on my knees before the Father, this magnificent Father who parcels out all heaven and earth. I ask him to strengthen you by his Spirit—not a brute strength but a glorious inner strength—that Christ will live in you as you open the door and invite him in. And I ask him that with both feet planted firmly on love, you'll be able to take in with all followers of Jesus the extravagant dimensions of Christ's love. Reach out and experience the breadth! Test its length! Plumb the depths! Rise to the heights! Live full lives, full in the fullness of God.
>
> Ephesians 3:14–19 MSG

devotional

Read Ephesians 3:1–21.

Paul felt like he was the least of all disciples. He didn't feel deserving of the wonderful privilege of sharing the gospel with the gentiles. Though his calling condemned him to be rejected, persecuted, shipwrecked, and finally beheaded for his faith, Paul felt privileged to serve Christ.

The tenacity of Paul was anchored in his ability to pray through difficult situations. When beaten and imprisoned, he responded with worship and hymns of praise. When in the middle of a storm, he comforted and instructed everyone around him. He tapped into the heavenly encouragement of God's presence.

There are times in our lives when there is nothing in our circumstance to bring us comfort. We need to go deeper and find comfort in God's love. Paul's response was to fall on his knees in prayer and ask God to strengthen him. He was firmly planted in the extravagant dimensions of Christ's love.

pray aloud

Magnificent Father, today I choose to be strengthened by your love and goodness. I want to know the extravagant dimensions of your love and grace. When I face difficult situations, help me to tenaciously persist with the truth of who you are.

declare

I am tenacious.

Day 19

Humility

One thing that every human being has in common is the struggle with pride. Describe a past or present situation in your life when you realized you were walking in pride.

So be content with who you are, and don't put on airs. God's strong hand is on you; he'll promote you at the right time. Live carefree before God; he is most careful with you.

1 Peter 5:6–7 MSG

Read 1 Peter 5:1–11.

God loves a humble heart. Jesus, God in flesh, modeled meekness. His strength was always constrained. He didn't show off or try to draw a crowd. Jesus continued to grow in favor with God and man as He walked humbly.

Since we know that "God resists the proud, but gives grace to the humble" (1 Peter 5:5 NKJV), we should have an internal guard on our heart against pride. But like so many sins of the flesh, we don't see it when we are walking in pride. It usually takes someone to show us our sin or for something to happen where we are confronted with it.

Peter describes humility as being "content with who you are." Only God is perfect, so we need to take ourselves off the hook when we fall short of God's best for our lives. Often, when the Holy Spirit is convicting us of sin, pride is involved. Pride is at the root of all sins.

If you want to be promoted, there is one simple thing you need to do—*humble yourself.* As you make yourself low, God will come in and establish His church. God's strong hand is already on your life. If you want to live a carefree life before God, walk in His humility.

pray aloud

Jesus, you amaze me. You are the One who has given so much. You made yourself of no reputation. You humbled yourself and became obedient even to death. I want to be like you. I choose to die to selfish pursuits and live fully alive for you. In Jesus' name, amen.

declare

I choose to be humble.

Day 20

Promotion

journal

Who does God promote? What precedes promotion? Describe a season of promotion in your life.

meditate

Pride first, then the crash, but humility is precursor to honor.

Proverbs 18:12 MSG

devotional

Read James 3:13–18 and James 4:1–10.

In our rock-star culture, it is a challenge talking about promotion. Promotion that comes from God leads to greater influence and responsibility. The Western church has become too impressed with fame. The celebrity culture has leaked into the way we think about godly promotion. God's Word calls us to "let someone else praise you, not your own mouth—a stranger, not your own lips" (Proverbs 27:2).

In a world of self-promotion, humility precedes promotion in God's kingdom: "True humility and fear of the Lord lead to riches, honor, and long life" (Proverbs 22:4). You can trust God to lead you and guide you in His ways. The way to promotion in God's kingdom is through humility.

You have a destiny in God that only you can fulfill. Aren't you glad that you don't have to make it happen? Isn't it wonderful that you can seek to serve God and others and that God will multiply your efforts by His Spirit? You can be yourself and walk freely in His presence without pressure to perform, push, or plan for your own personal success and promotion. You can trust God to lead you and guide you and promote you with His mighty hand.

pray aloud

Forgiving God, cleanse me of every form of self-promotion. Create within the soil of my heart a culture of servanthood. I trust you to promote me to serve and help others. Make me a messenger of your love and transformation. I want to be famous in heaven, so I choose humility here on earth. In Jesus' name, amen.

declare

I am famous in heaven.

Day 21

Favor

What does God's favor in your life look like?

> Never let loyalty and kindness leave you! Tie them around your neck as a reminder. Write them deep within your heart. Then you will find favor with both God and people, and you will earn a good reputation.
>
> Proverbs 3:3–4

Read Luke 4:16–19.

As you walk humbly with God and build loyalty in your relationships, you will find favor with both God and people. Your gifts and talents are perfectly suited for His destiny in your life. He walks with you as you go through your day. He turns the mundane into the miraculous.

You have been created with a one-of-a-kind destiny. God's Spirit is on you. He has anointed you and appointed you as an agent of transformation. You carry God's message in your life. You are a carrier of His presence. He is using you to bring good news to the poor and freedom to the bound and recovery to the blind.

Learn to sense His favor on you, His gentle, quiet, powerful presence leading you and guiding you. His ways are higher than your ways (Isaiah 55:9).

pray aloud

God, awaken my senses to how you are already using me to touch others. I choose to be loyal to you and to all whom you have called me to serve. I trust you, God, with my reputation. Thank you for your favor that helps me do what you have called me to do. I choose to look at life the way you do. I am ready and available to you. Mold me. Fill me. Use me. In your name, amen.

declare

I have God's favor.

Guidelines for Taking a Spiritual Retreat

Choose a day during the next few weeks to get alone with God. Shut off your computer and social media and just be with God. Take your Bible, a journal, and this book and focus your heart and mind to listen. You can book a hotel room to stay in so that you will be undistracted, or you can make your home into a retreat center.

On this retreat you are going to concentrate on the following areas:

1. Relationship with God
2. Purpose in life
3. Family
4. Relationships
5. Work

I know that these are not all of the areas of your life, and God may speak to you about other things while you wait on Him. God may bring up unresolved or painful issues from your past and help you to see things with His fresh perspective. He may just want you to rest and take a day of Sabbath with your journal in hand. If you set aside the time and purpose to seek God with all of your heart, you will find Him and hear His voice.

Relationship with God

Pray this prayer out loud:

God, I have been made to know you. Today, I am choosing freshly to make you first in my life. I am turning away from everything that has distracted me from you in the past. I know that as I draw close to you, you will draw close to me. I'm trusting you that I will hear your voice. Jesus, I am declaring that you are the Lord of my life. Thank you for giving me the Holy Spirit. Take me deeper in my relationship with you, beginning today. It's in your name that I pray. Amen.

Write down a prayer from your heart to God. After your prayer, read aloud the following Scripture promises.

Scripture Promises

I am a woman of faith (Romans 12:3).

I will come toward His light (John 1:5).

I will seek God diligently (Hebrews 11:6).

God rewards me with His favor (Hebrews 11:6).

I am confident that He will complete His work in me (Philippians 1:6).

My prayers are powerful (James 5:16).

God answers my prayers (John 14:13).

I trust God (Proverbs 3:5).

I will walk in faith (2 Corinthians 5:7).

I am chosen (Colossians 3:12).

I am a joy and delight to my heavenly Father (Proverbs 10:1).

I am adopted as His heir (Ephesians 1:5).

I am the apple of His eye (Psalm 17:8).

In my weakness God is strong (2 Corinthians 12:10).

I can do all things through Christ who strengthens me (Philippians 4:13).

I am a new creation in Christ (2 Corinthians 5:17).

My joy comes from God's presence (Psalm 16:11).

He has already empowered me to be free from sin (Romans 3:24).

I can be close to God (James 4:8).

He is my healer (Exodus 15:26).

I walk in God's grace (1 Peter 1:2).

I have God's favor (Proverbs 3:4).

I am free from sin (Psalm 18:23).

I will fulfill my destiny (Ephesians 2:10).

God will fulfill His promises (Romans 4:20).

I hope in God (Psalm 43:5).

I trust God's Word (1 John 2:5).

I walk in peace (Philippians 4:7).

I am an overcomer (Romans 12:21).

I am filled with His joy (Psalm 28:7).

I humble myself (Romans 12:3).

I am courageous (Joshua 1:6).

I am bold (Psalm 138:3).

I am fearless (2 Timothy 1:7).

I am hopeful (1 Corinthians 13:7).

I am transformed (Romans 12:2).

Purpose

Pray this prayer out loud:

God, you have created me with purpose. You have uniquely gifted me with a plan in mind. I'm taking time to listen to you speak about that plan right now.

1. **Past Promises:** *Remind me of those promises that you have spoken in the past.* Write down things that God has called you to in the past.

2. **Present Promises:** *Restore the passion in my heart for those promises that I am in the middle of walking out.* Write down the things He has called you to in the present.

3. **Future Promises:** *Surprise me, God, with your purpose for my future.* Write down the things He is calling you to in the future.

4. **Letting Go of the Past:** *God, I trust your Word, which says, "Not that I have already attained, or am already perfected; but I press on, that I may lay hold of that for which Christ Jesus has also laid hold of me. Brethren, I do not count myself to have apprehended; but one thing I do, forgetting those things which are behind and reaching forward to those things which are ahead, I press toward the goal for the prize of the upward call of God in Christ Jesus" (Philippians 3:12–14* NKJV).

   God, what things do I need to let go of from my past in order to walk into my future? Help me to even let go of the good things in order to walk into your best. I'm listening, Lord. Speak to me. Write down what you hear God saying.

Family

Pray this prayer out loud:

> *Thank you, God, for the gift of my home and family. I know that you have a special plan for my family to serve you and make you known. Thank you for each relationship. Show me how I can walk in honor and health with each member of my family.*

Write down each member of your family and take time to listen to God about your relationship. Write down significant things you hear God say.

Relationships

Pray this prayer out loud:

> *Thank you, Lord Jesus, for creating me to be in relationship with others. I know that when I am full of your love, grace, truth, and mercy, that I have good things to give others in my life. Show me the key relationships that you want me to nurture in the days ahead. Help me walk in love and respect. Free me from toxic relationships and help me to walk in greater health in how I relate to others.*

Write down your key relationships and listen to God. Invite the Holy Spirit to speak into how you relate to others.

Work

Pray this prayer out loud:

> *God, I pray that you would use the work that I do to bring your light to others. Thank you for your provision in the past. Lord, I am listening freshly about my work. Do you have any changes that you would like me to make? Expand my thinking to see the work that I do from your perspective.*

Write down what you hear God saying.

Guidelines for Fasting

I struggled with whether to include a section on fasting in *Women Who Move Mountains*. Knowing the tendency of some of us women to try to meet legalist religious standards, I did not want to communicate that if you don't fast you aren't spiritual.

Jesus is our best model for prayer. Even though the Holy Spirit led Him to begin His ministry with forty days of fasting in the wilderness (Mark 1:11–13), He didn't let the Pharisees bully His disciples into regimented fasting.

This is how Jesus responded to their questions:

> Once when John's disciples and the Pharisees were fasting, some people came to Jesus and asked, "Why don't your disciples fast like John's disciples and the Pharisees do?" Jesus replied, "Do wedding guests fast while celebrating with the groom? Of course not. They can't fast while the groom is with them. But someday the groom will be taken away from them, and then they will fast."
>
> Mark 2:18–20

I love how Jesus refused to be trapped. He both affirmed the season of celebrating His presence on earth and pointed to a time after His death and resurrection when His disciples would fast.

I chose to include this section on fasting because it has been a powerful part of my prayer life. I have fasted in many different

248

ways during my walk with God. There have been times when I have begun a fast only to quit it on the same day. I found that I needed to be clear whether it was the Holy Spirit calling me to a fast or my flesh trying to religiously perform. I found that I can only fast with the grace of God leading me and guiding me.

The benefits I have found from fasting include:

Clarity for decision making

Focusing on hearing God's voice

Repenting from sin

Interceding for difficult situations

Detoxing my body, mind, and spirit

Letting go of the past and embracing the present and future

Healing and rest

Interceding for national and global causes

I hope this guide is helpful to you if you choose to fast.

How to Begin Your Fast

This Scripture captivated my heart when I first chose to fast:

> If my people, who are called by my name, will humble themselves and pray and seek my face and turn from their wicked ways, then I will hear from heaven, and I will forgive their sin and will heal their land.
>
> 2 Chronicles 7:14 NIV

The foundation of every fast includes a call to humble yourself and to pray. As you confess your desperate need for God, He will hear you. As you fast you are acknowledging that God's ways are higher than your ways. You are choosing to turn away from the often hidden and deceptive ways of the world. You unclutter your mind and heart to hear from God. You surrender your own agenda and purpose to embrace God's perspective.

Why Are You Fasting?

If you believe that the Holy Spirit is leading you to a fast, here are a few helpful questions to answer as you begin: What do you hope to gain from your fast? Are you fasting for spiritual direction? Do you feel led to fast and pray for your children or marriage? Are you praying for a difficult situation to be resolved? Ask the Holy Spirit to clarify the purpose of your fast. Being purposeful with your fast will help you complete it.

What Kind of Fast?

There are many types of fasts. It's helpful to ask the Holy Spirit to guide you in how to fast. Also, seek a medical doctor's advice. Here are a few ideas for fasting as you use the *21 Days to Spiritual Breakthrough*:

Media Fast: You could fast from television and social media for twenty-one days to create space in your mind and heart to hear God.

Daniel Fast: You could abstain from eating meat and concentrate on eating vegetables for twenty-one days.

Liquid Fast: You could choose to drink juices or protein shakes during the twenty-one days.

One-Meal Fast: You could choose to fast one meal a day and spend that time in prayer during the twenty-one days of prayer and fasting.

One-Day Fast: You could decide to fast from eating one day a week for a total of three days in the next twenty-one days.

21-Day Fast: If you have spent time abstaining from food through fasting in the past, you could choose to fast all food for the next twenty-one days. If this is the case, please seek medical confirmation that you are healthy enough to fast from food during the twenty-one days. You will need to drink a great deal of water and prepare for your body to be weak.

Will I Experience Increased Spiritual Conflict?

Every day we experience some form of spiritual conflict, but we may not always recognize it. Scripture makes it clear:

> Our struggle is not against flesh and blood, but against the rulers, against the authorities, against the powers of this dark world and against the spiritual forces of evil in the heavenly realms.
>
> Ephesians 6:12 NIV

Fasting may make you more aware of the spiritual conflict that you are in, but it won't necessarily increase it. One of the things I like about fasting is that I feel a greater freedom from temptation. One of the benefits of fasting is that it puts your fleshly appetites under your feet.

Fasting can help you break addictions in your life. This Scripture is encouraging:

> Is this not the fast that I have chosen: To loose the bonds of wickedness, to undo the heavy burdens, to let the oppressed go free, and that you break every yoke? Is it not to share your bread with the hungry, and that you bring to your house the poor who are cast out; when you see the naked, that you cover him, and not hide yourself from your own flesh? Then your light shall break forth like the morning, your healing shall spring forth speedily, and your righteousness shall go before you; the glory of the Lord shall be your rear guard. Then you shall call, and the Lord will answer; you shall cry, and He will say, "Here I am."
>
> Isaiah 58:6–9 NKJV

Fasting helps you to break off yokes from yourself and others. It helps you to look more deeply and evaluate your life from God's perspective. It helps you to get rid of heavy burdens and lighten your emotional baggage. Fasting provides you an opportunity to call on God and hear His answer to your cry.

How Do I Prepare for a Fast?

Do not rush into your fast. Ask the Holy Spirit to prepare you physically, spiritually, and emotionally. Fasting can make you cranky as your body and soul detoxes. The first two or three days are the most difficult.

Schedule your day to make room for God to speak. You may begin your day by playing your favorite worship music. Take walks and talk with God. Have an unhurried pace to your life.

Read and meditate on God's Word and use the twenty-one-day devotional to guide you.

As you fast, remember you are not trying to twist the arm of God to give you what you want. Fasting has more to do with humbling yourself before God so that you are able to hear His voice more clearly. Fasting will help your spiritual hunger become stronger.

Fasting for Spiritual Breakthrough

If Jesus is our model for prayer, we need to remember that His forty-day fast began a season of people being healed and delivered. He overcame the Enemy and has made a way for you and me to do the same. A spiritual breakthrough is when we break through the Enemy's camp and invade the Enemy's territory. Fasting and prayer will help you take ground in your spiritual journey.

As you move forward in faith, anticipate that you will be transformed in the midst of your walk with God. He will draw you closer to himself. *Ask the Holy Spirit to lead and guide you on this spiritual journey.*

NOTES

Chapter 1: I Believe, Transforming Fear into Faith

1. The story of the fire is from Sue Detweiler, *9 Traits of a Life-Giving Mom* (New York: Morgan James, 2014), 1–4. Used by permission.
2. See Hebrews 11:6.

Chapter 5: I Am Healed, Transforming Brokenness into Wholeness

1. The flask is also called a jar or box in different translations. It was made of alabaster and held precious fragrant oil that was often part of a dowry. It was also used to anoint someone's body to prepare them for burial.
2. Eliezer Segal, "Who Has Not Made Me a Woman," *My Jewish Learning*, www.myjewishlearning.com/article/who-has-not-made-me-a-woman.

Chapter 7: I Am Honored, Transforming Shame into Grace

1. John Newton, "Amazing Grace," Public Domain.
2. David Sheward, "The Real Story Behind 'Amazing Grace,'" Biography.com, August 11, 2015, www.biography.com/news/amazing-grace-story-john-newton.

Chapter 8: Learning to Pray with Grace

1. Rick Renner, *Sparkling Gems* (Tulsa, OK: Harrison House, 2003), 377–80.

Chapter 9: I Am Secure, Transforming Anxiety into Peace

1. This story is from Sue Detweiler, *9 Traits of a Life-Giving Mom* (New York: Morgan James, 2014), 1–4. Used by permission.
2. This story is from Sue Detweiler, *9 Traits of a Life-Giving Mom* (New York: Morgan James, 2014), 40–41. Used by permission.

3. Taken from Sue Detweiler, *9 Traits of a Life-Giving Mom* (New York: Morgan James, 2014), 41–42. Used by permission.

Chapter 10: Learning to Pray with Peace

1. Jack W. Hayford et al., *Spirit-Filled Life Bible* (Nashville: Thomas Nelson, 2002, 2013), 661.

2. Ibid., 764.

3. "Psalm 37," *The Bible Hub,* http://biblehub.com/commentaries/psalms /37-1.htm.

4. Jack W. Hayford et al., *Spirit-Filled Life Bible,* 1206.

5. Wilma Mankiller, AZ Quotes, http://www.azquotes.com/author/9385-Wilma _Mankiller.

Chapter 11: I Am Transformed, Transforming Sadness into Joy

1. From Sue Detweiler, *9 Traits of a Life-Giving Mom* (New York: Morgan James, 2014), 23–24. This section used with permission.

Chapter 15: I Am Humble, Transforming Entitlement into Humility

1. Dietrich Bonhoeffer, *The Cost of Discipleship,* 99.

2. Mary Demuth, "God, Success, and Failed French Church Plants," Wrecked. org, August 21, 2010, www.wrecked.org/church/god-success-and-failed-french -church-plants.

3. Jean M. Twenge and W. Keith Campbell, *The Narcissism Epidemic: Living in the Age of Entitlement* (New York: Simon & Schuster, 2009), 1.

Chapter 19: I Am Expectant, Transforming Disappointment and Loss into Hope

1. Jack W. Hayford et al., *The Spirit-Filled Life Bible* (Nashville: Thomas Nelson, 2002, 2013), 1536.

Chapter 20: Learning to Pray with Hope

1. David Kessler and Elisabeth Kübler-Ross, *On Grief and Grieving* (New York: Simon & Schuster, 2005).

ABOUT THE AUTHOR

Sue Detweiler is a wife, mom, radio host, and pastor with more than twenty-five years of experience in marriage, ministry, and education. She is also a popular speaker who shares her heart and wisdom internationally on issues related to marriage, family, women, prayer, leadership, and ministry.

Sue's first book, *9 Traits of a Life-Giving Mom,* hit No. 1 on Amazon's hot new releases for Christian women's issues. Her second book, *9 Traits of a Life-Giving Marriage,* grew out of her and her husband's heart to help couples grow closer to God and to each other. In their pastoral ministry, they have seen how sharing their own struggles has helped to create a safe context for individuals and couples to be transparent and honest with their issues. Wayne and Sue have also seen God's transformative power heal and restore lives through the conferences and workshops they have led. For more books and resources or to schedule a speaking engagement, visit SueDetweiler.com or email info@suedetweiler.com.

Background

Sue responded to God's call on her life out of heartfelt obedience to what the Bible commands. Sue and her husband, Wayne, began in ministry as youth pastors. They moved to Nashville in 1986 and planted and pastored Harmony Christian Fellowship for nine years. During this time, Sue received her Master of Divinity degree from Vanderbilt University. Sue and Wayne became a part of The Foursquare Church through their roles as associate pastors at New Song Christian Fellowship. Sue had the privilege of overseeing Life School of Ministry, a Bible training program, which helps students develop their ministry gifts. She was also the principal at New Song Christian Academy, a homeschool program for kindergarten through eighth grade. Sue partnered with her husband, Wayne, in marriage ministry and led prayer locally and citywide. Sue and Wayne have relocated north of Dallas, Texas, to plant and pastor Life Bridge Church, where everyone is welcome, no one is perfect, and anything is possible with God!

Connect with Sue:

Twitter: @SueDetweiler
Facebook: Facebook.com/SueDetweiler7
Linkedin: Linkedin.com/in/suedetweiler
Pinterest: Pinterest.com/SueDetweiler
Online: SueDetweiler.com and LifeBridgeChurch4.com